Unequal Partnership:

A dating guide for loving non-egalitarian relationships

Aisha-Sky Gates

Published and distributed in the United States by IngramSpark

Book cover photography by James Arana

Library of Congress Cataloging-in-Publication Data

Gates, Aisha-Sky

Unequal Partnership: a dating guide for loving non-egalitarian relationships/ Aisha-Sky Gates.

1st printing. July, 2017

ISBN-10: 0-692-91205-3

ISBN-13: 978-0-692-91205-8 (paperback)

ASIN: B06Y5PH18P
released April 2017

Printed in the United States of America

Acknowledgements

I love my wonderful S-type partner. I thank him for our amazing years thus far, for his patience and understanding, and for his talented Everyman editing skills.

Table of Contents

Introduction . . . .　5

One: The Unequal Partnership . . . .　15

Two: Power and Control in a Relationship . . . .　53

Three: Now, Let's Do Some Dating . . . .　67

Four: The Dating Pool & Dating Strategies . . . .　88

Five: You Can Find Your Leading Partner . . . .　105

Six: You Can Find Your Implementing Partner . . . . .　112

Seven: A Few Dating Snafus and Combinations . . .　121

Eight: Dating Went Well . . . .　128

Nine: Deeper Negotiations . . . .　147

Conclusion: Loving with Structured Walls . . . .　152

About the Author . . . .　156

Addendum 1 . . . .　157

Addendum 2 . . . .　161

List of Resources . . . .　164

Endnotes . . . .　166

Introduction

This is the first book. It is an unusual dating guide with a specialized target audience. I want to talk to anyone who

---Wants a loving, long term relationship,

---Wants a non-egalitarian relationship that's an informed choice,

---And wants a relationship that honors and respects and empowers all partners.

It is the first in a series that explains the Unequal Partnership, my model of one kind of structured hierarchical relationship. I know it's a mouthful but that's just a category name. My model is called Unequal Partnership. People who practice it call themselves unequal partners or Unequal Partnership couples. But if you are not sure that you are in these waters that's okay. Keep reading. I'll explain everything. I have loaded up every page with good wisdom for all who are dating.

You'll discover that I am not trying to sell my thinking to anyone or convince you that a hierarchical relationship is the way to go for your life. It's for some, not all. Some will find that the model fits them naturally and that's what is required. No one can role-play the attitudes, values, and behaviors described here. It won't work. Only a natural fit will do. While it's not for everyone, thousands of families have found their deep, profound happiness through the practice of a non-egalitarian relationship. Unequal Partnership is one non-egalitarian way to live.

Relationships are a lot of work and they can be deliberately planned, beginning with the dating phase. Deliberate steps during dating can guide what you'll need relationship-wise toward stability and sustainability. "We love each other and, therefore, we commit to being together" isn't enough of a plan if you want to stay together and be happy for the long haul.

Romantic love does not stand up well in the face of all the decision-making that must be done in a normal life. If you love each other then I am very happy for you. But now what do you do? Bills have to be paid, children have to be planned for or decided against, seeking more education means organizing time and effort and probably some sacrifices, a home has to be maintained, and laundry has to get done and food prepared by someone. Conclusion: be deliberate in your choices about how the relationship will be conducted. Wow. Can relationship organization be chosen upfront? Yes. There are choices? Yes. By choosing and committing to the roles, the protocols, and behaviors that are best for you, you can avoid a great deal of relationship grief. But more than that, a great deal of happiness and personal development can be provided and maintained in the home that you create with your beloved.

If you want a loving, sustainable relationship then you must start building now, while you are dating. Your everyday life must contain positive attitudes, attention to what's needed to get you to your goal, and actual activity that makes it all happen. I know you thought that you could lie back and, at most, concentrate on what to wear on your next date. You can. You can if that's all that you want.

Partnering is what I teach. I happen to be a relationship coach of ten-plus years. Partnering is not the simpler arrangement of merely cohabiting or delightfully coexisting until . . . well, until. Lots of couples make committed arrangements with the best of intentions but without a model for partnership. Not everyone wants partnership anyway; it's just too much responsibility some would say. That's okay. But for those of you who would like to consider a partnership in your future allow me to offer

1. My super special Unequal Partnership model plus
2. A guide for how to prepare yourself to enter an Unequal Partnership plus
3. An explanation of what to look for as you date.

Everyone begins with what I call the Boyfriend/girlfriend scenario. It's the omnipresent case that gets sold to everyone. Just turn the television on randomly or go to a romantic comedy movie or look at the high book sales for romance novels. Boy meets girl. After a serious of obstacles that they must overcome—and they do--they are always joyously in love at the end of the book or the movie or the TV show. The scenario says that their love is enough to see them through whatever life throws at them. Boy and his Girl have Love but nothing got decided about how they would live together. No agreements were made or there were few. Most likely lots of implicit agreements were made like who cooks and how often but where were the deliberate, above the table agreements that gave structure to how they would proceed with their life together? How about deliberate attention given to making sure that both partners are fully empowered to give consent to all of their decisions? Where will they live and who will take care of their finances and the children and the laundry? No one ever asked what they each want to get from a marriage or other committed arrangement. What are their shared goals and why? Partnership requires structure that the two partners create to meet their needs and theirs alone. The partners have one overarching reason for being together: they are aimed at creating their personal happiness. They work to make all that happen without any assumptions that love alone will bring them the happiness that they desire.

Lots of people make lots of assumptions about what a committed relationship is going to be like. They assume that their special person with whom they get along so well has a similar worldview as their own and similar values. Chances are your mental picture of commitment and theirs, as well, is strongly influenced by television, movies, video games, and other forms of popular culture. As life situations arise, Girl and Boy with Love in Their Pockets might discover who is best at decision making, who is best at follow through during tough times, and how they relate to each other when things aren't easy. Will they develop a means for deriving best practices and best decisions for their family? Will they remember to protect each other's feelings when they have disagreements? Those are heavy loads to leave to chance with on-the-fly decisions. Couples have a much better chance of answering yes if <u>inclusive decision making</u> and <u>agreement pacts</u> are the foundation of their relationship. Unequal Partnership is one well-tested relationship mode of choice for couples that want long term sustainability. Unequal Partnership necessitates persistent work on such a foundation.

I promised that this is a dating guidebook. What's at issue is how exactly can someone conduct dating in a specific or more focused way. The goal is to find their non-egalitarian mate who wants to commit to an Unequal Partnership. The objectives toward that goal are

1. To prepare yourself to be in an Unequal Partnership and

2. To be able to recognize mate possibilities while dating.

This text will tutor you in the Unequal Partnership model so that you know what you're attempting to move toward as you date, that is, if deliberately Unequal is going to be your way to live. Remember, Unequal Partnership is the right and wonderful relationship mode that suits some, not all.

There's a chapter on what to avoid while dating. You'll enjoy the discussion about power and control in relationships.

Next, there's how to prepare yourself for the Unequal Partnership. You are going to begin to think of yourself as an Unequal partner right now. You are an Unequal partner looking for your Unequal mate. As such, you might need to learn a new skill or two, reading lots of good literature is always a good idea for making sure that you are a sparkling conversationalist, and you might want to use your dating opportunities to practice being an attentive, generous of heart, intelligent, and caring partner.

Then, you'll want lots of information about how to identify your beloved Unequal partner.

The book concludes with a big chapter on negotiation. If a couple is to be successful long-term then they must incorporate agreement-making as a normal part of relationship business. The Unequal Partnership model believes in negotiating upfront and happily expecting to negotiate again and again as needed through the years of commitment to each other. Negotiating how to live as a working partnership is in itself a lifelong commitment.

Many of my relationship clients are Unequal Partnership couples or individuals who are working their way toward such a partnership. I am grateful to every one of them for their personal sharing and for their instructive questions. Just between you and me, on the personal side, I am delighted to share that I am in a healthy, happy Unequal Partnership.

Unequal Partnerships are healthy, mindfully conducted non-egalitarian intimate relationships. They are aimed at fulfilling the needs of both partners. It is my pleasure and my duty to tell the world about them. It makes me very happy to think about any and all partnership topics, to write about a relationship mode that is only just beginning to have a literature, and it is exciting to me to join many other counselors, therapists, psychologists, and health professionals who are discussing Unequal Partnerships and spreading credible information about them.

But let's get back to you in particular. If you are into ethical, caring hierarchies in your personal life then you probably already understand that you are different from the general dating crowd. You want a life partner who is strongly committed to a non-egalitarian relationship. That's in addition to commitment to building a long-term sustainable loving relationship . . . with you. That's pretty darn specific but so rewarding once you get there. Consider what you have to offer a potential mate, as well. Then, date. Have fun. Think of dating as your own personal system of discovery. You're learning about your prospective mate. The right person will make <u>your</u> needs a high priority. That's what partners do. Your goal should be to settle into a non-egalitarian <u>partnership</u>. As you date, always be headed toward negotiations. Negotiations officially mark the beginning of a wonderful structured (agreement-made) relationship.

Last, let me say that even if you are reading this book just because you are curious and you discover that Unequal

Partnership isn't for you then I promise you that still your time will have been well spent. Ultimately, this is a book about building a healthy, sustainable, committed loving relationship and you wouldn't want to miss out on that.

Chapter One:
The Unequal Partnership

The Unequal Partnership is one form of non-egalitarian relationship. I present it here as just one of many ways to organize, govern, and maintain a committed intimate relationship. The partners have an alternative arrangement with no attempt at traditional equality. One partner is accepted and respected as leading. One partner is accepted and respected as implementing. Decision making is inclusive but not equal. Their shared and united purpose is to create a structured (agreement-based) home environment that provides for all needs. But why? What do the partners believe that structuring the nest will bring them? Personal happiness. Otherwise, why be together? Commitment to each other by this model begins with planning. For an Unequal Partnership couple, planning is the hallmark activity that ensures their long-term stability.

Unequal Partnership is the unique name for my relationship model. The name sums up the philosophy of the model. I've written here about a non-egalitarian arrangement of power for couples wanting a long-term sustainable relationship. Every aspect of this power sharing arrangement is consensual. The aim of their carefully constructed slant on power in the relationship is partnership and through partnership they expect to net their personal happiness. Any intimate relationship that has an intention of long-term sustainability faces a heavy load of responsibility. An Unequal Partnership has a deliberate placement of responsibilities from the very beginning. Why wait until Life presents problems, hurdles, or tragedies before plans of action are discussed? Unequal Partnership couples are living with the bones of the relationship already formed by their agreements upfront and throughout their years together.

My description may sound like all work and no fun but that would be far, far from the beautiful romantic reality that thousands of couples are living and loving every day. Each partner is expressing their committed love by faithfully fulfilling their responsibilities. Partners are expressing who they really are by doing a good job as the leading partner or the implementing partner. And that is a crucial point. The partners are just being themselves. Their leader or implementer roles give them the best possible conditions for expressing their true nature. With a beloved mate gazing at them adoringly they each feel emboldened to be themselves. True Nature is a core concept of Unequal Partnership. You and I have such a thing as True Nature. It's our Innermost Self that---if we listen---will give us clues about who I am and how to steer the life that I was given. What do I really need? What is most satisfying to me? What most deeply moves me? In what way is my life to be in service?

Hierarchy exists in almost all intimate relationships.[1] Please do not assume that hierarchy in relationships means no love, no romance. Or, that hierarchy must mean one person controlling another. No and no. Sure, it's a common thing to discover that a couple began an egalitarian relationship but over time power and control slanted toward one of them. At some level, of course, each of them understands that this is what has happened. Over time one of them ceded a little power and then a little more. It just seemed easier to give in. One of them might have been more vocal and more assertive or aggressive and accustomed to getting their way. That domineering person may think that their choices are best for the couple as a whole. That's what they tell themselves. The other person is just capitulating. Capitulation feels terrible and yet may be associated with being loved. These conditions are disempowering. Love, respect, and partnering are missing. These unconscious conditions are not what I mean when I say that an Unequal Partnership is non-egalitarian. There is nothing unconscious about an Unequal Partnership.

Hierarchy refers to two things. First, it implies that the two positions for the partners are **unequal**, <u>defined as not identical in power or responsibilities</u>. That's perfectly acceptable in the Unequal Partnership model because everything from conception to design to agreement and application in their lives is consensual. One of the partners is given some extra degree of control in the decision making process and in an Unequal Partnership this is completely consensual. The purpose of this mindful and fully consensual slant on power and control in the relationship is to give the leading partner the ability to act in the couple's interest according to the leading partner's completely agreed upon set of responsibilities. The implementing partner is empowered by being freed of responsibilities that they would rather not take on and empowered by being free to concentrate on the responsibilities that best suit them. The two partners complement each other in their set of responsibilities and so much more. Secondly, hierarchy implies different status for the two relationship positions. That's not acceptable in an Unequal Partnership. In an Unequal Partnership the two partners hold the same honored status. Hierarchy in this model has no One Down Position.

Power. An Unequal Partnership is all about good continuous communication, most especially where power is concerned. This kind of partnership has the partners deliberately planning and agreeing on how to conduct their lives. Both partners are the holders of power but there is an additional amount allocated to the partner in lead position to be used for the good of the couple or family unit. There is no despot or demigod in residence. No one is One Up on anyone and there is no one in a One Down position to be exploited. There is only a partner, someone who takes her responsibilities very seriously, whether leading or implementing. Each partner puts the other's needs first in their thinking, knowing for certain that their own needs will be met as well. Power is not held exclusively by either partner or used to promote one person's ego. Power does not get used to consolidate power. Instead, power gets disbursed throughout the relationship for the good of the couple as a whole.

Egalitarian. I'll give you my best talk about attempting an egalitarian relationship. Americans via polls say they want egalitarian relationships. That's what they want. Research says that the more support that a couple has (paid leave, elder care, child care) the more serious both men and women are about working to maintain an egalitarian relationship structure.[2] But, of course, American society at present offers very little support for working families. That fact alone contributes persistent stress on the love and commitment that all types of couples try very hard to maintain for themselves.

Egalitarian. I had to explain this concept to a dear friend of mine. "Egalitarianism" in an intimate relationship is understood as a belief system that says that there should be an equal split in finances and in domestic responsibilities. As such there is a visual and continuous assurance that power and control in the relationship are split equally. Given that understanding, if Americans are asked to imagine that which is not egalitarian they can only say to themselves NOT-equal, something is not equal. Some arrangement with my love relationship is NOT EQUAL. "Not equal" means a possible abuse situation? "Not equal" means not loved? "Not equal" means somebody is being taken advantage of? Call a therapist. Call the police.

What's the underlying issue here? Let's find out by examining a common situation that isn't necessarily intimate but could be. How about two people dining together and the question is who pays? Well, the answer can be an even split. Sure. Fifty-fifty. Each can walk away without feeling loss. Each person can feel right and righteous and not taken advantage of. That's key. Not feeling like a chump ranks high with Americans, even in their personal lives. It's key because the real issue is fairness. Each person is protective of self. In dating or as part of a relationship, each of us wants to be sure that we have been treated fairly. How do we do that? How do you think about fairness?

In my restaurant scenario there are fairness options:
---Paying 50-50,
---Paying an unequal amount that's agreed upon. There has to be a compelling reason to justify an uneven payout though or someone is going to feel cheated.
---Reciprocity. "I'll pay it today. You pay for our meal

next time." "Okay. Great."

Most modern couples have the burden or joy of supporting two careers. Even if one of them sets the career aside to stay at home and care for children or a parent they probably have near-future potential of being a two-income family. I am guessing that such an income-abled home climate breeds an expectation of reciprocity. Without mutually held rules and protocols around money issues reciprocity becomes the default expectation. With agreements about money in place then reciprocity still is probably the cultural default but now issues are manageable.

Let me be clear and say that the concept of fairness has no objective definition in reality. Instead, it's a private determination made by the partners of any sort. They are the ones who have to feel right about what is fair to each of them. Believe me, this is no small matter. Singularly, the partners have to feel good and right. There's that thing again: each wants to feel that they have been treated fairly. Okay. So, the reciprocity method probably covers the big items for the couple like how many times a week the partners can afford to eat out, how to get the bills paid, and how to save for a trip to the Caribbean.

It's easy to imagine that the couple that has such an important agreement between them about money matters cannot help but to extend their feelings about fairness to domestic issues like their sexual activities and who takes out the trash or who cooks meals. Laundry might be on that list. In these matters, their feelings speak for them. Those feelings say that if the agreement is 50/50 with public activities like going out to eat then surely there is no reason to set different rules about private activities. It's 50/50 all around and all the way through, right?

But what if it isn't? What if in reality some things can be maintained at 50/50 but other things like care, kindness, and how much attention each person gets do not fit neatly into the Equal Every Moment expectation. What if one partner remarkably needs cuddling and to be listened to much more than the other partner? Is that person sucking up more than their share on the Equality/Fairness meter? Does each partner need to measure out a certain amount of sexual satisfaction and no more, just to be fair? Life doesn't work that way as far as I am aware. Over time, what would you say is likely to happen? Couples, sometime, walk into horrendous fights because of an expectation of fairness that is being mitigated via reciprocity. Each person feels right and righteous and I can understand why.

In my opinion and in my professional experience our hypothetical couple is not going to stay egalitarian over time. Time is the in-your-face element that wears on people. Over time, power and control in an intimate relationship leans in the direction of one of the partners. Perhaps, it is a slight slant or a much stronger degree of power and control favoring one of them. It happens. Very few couples can ever stay truly egalitarian but, yes, there are some.

If egalitarianism slips then what do you think happens with this business of reciprocity? Well, somebody is likely to use their stronger degree of control to make sure that he or she gets their pound and a half out of the relationship. Still, the One Up person may or may not be happy no matter what they are receiving. Sometimes, either partner is likely to sneak to get what they believe is their due. Probably, the One Down person isn't getting what they believe is fair and they resent it. I knew a wife who told me that she had no expectation of telling her husband everything: "you have to keep some things to yourself." That wife was likely to sneak and keep some purchases in her car trunk for quite some time. I knew another wife who wasn't getting as much emotional connection at home as she needed so her co-worker surreptitiously had taken on that responsibility. In these unfortunate scenarios, conversations about getting one's needs met usually happen only when one or both partners are quite emotional about <u>not</u> getting their needs met and <u>not</u> feeling fairly treated. Where are the positive and calm conversations that result in agreements about how to use their resources to meet each person's needs? Where is the couple's commitment to attempting to meet <u>both</u> partners' needs on a continuous basis?

An Alternative Notion of What is Fair. At this point, I am betting that it would not be much of a stretch to turn our attention to fairness in an Unequal Partnership. Unequal partners create and maintain fairness by aiming themselves toward equity, not equality.

Recently, I saw a poster that graphically explained "equality" versus "equity."[3] Stylized drawings of people are standing on boxes in order to see a ball game on the other side of a wall. Since, in this scene, distribution was mandated to be equal each person has received the same size box. However, the three persons are not the same height. More height gives someone an advantage to be able to see over the fence. That's the equality case. Everyone is given the same amount of any given resource; that's the measure for fairness. Remember, by this way of thinking, we must begin with an insistence of fairness. Fairness becomes the upfront-and-always goal to reach. Equal distribution of resources is the chosen vehicle for delivering fairness <u>and</u> the measure of success. If it's equal then it must be fair. But what happens to the unasked question of whether each person received what he or she needed?

Now, what about equity? If the goal is to make sure that everyone can see the game on the other side of the fence—meeting each person's need---then we need to give each person a box that's the right size to compensate for their particular height. The taller person gets a shorter box than a shorter person who needs to receive a taller box. The point is to make sure that everybody gets to see the game. That's the question to ask: did everyone get their needs met? That's the question that an Unequal Partner would constantly hold as most important. Meeting needs becomes the measure of fairness.

Unequal Partners make deliberate, agreed upon assignments of resources (the height of the boxes but also other elements like bringing water for themselves and enough to share). As the relationship goes forward (that is, as the game goes on and they are observers) the couple (the people standing on the boxes) check on each other and make whatever modifications that need to be made (like adjusting the position of the boxes, distributing food or more water during the game). The only goal, and it is a shared one, is the happiness of the participants. I think my analogy works best if we regard the people on the boxes as having agency in their lives and, specifically, in the pursuit of their own happiness. For instance, they probably brought their own food so that they are eating exactly what would please them. Perhaps, the equality dictate would garner them the same number of sandwiches of the same sort for each person. Otherwise, someone might feel cheated because equality is the determinant of fair treatment. As agents in their own lives the Unequal Partners are likely to innovate: maybe, additionally, they brought chairs for their comfort. Maybe they constructed boxes that were wide enough to perch a chair on top. Of course, Unequal Partners would think to check on each other's comfort throughout the game.

In an Unequal Partnership fairness is certainly desired. It is part of any pursuit of personal happiness. But the goal where asset allocation or distribution of resources or delivery of personal services is concerned is always <u>meeting all needs (in pursuit of happiness)</u>. I want to make sure that my partner's needs are met first and foremost. My partner is thinking the same in my direction. The Unequal Partners are assessing their needs all the time. Equity is the concept that is used as the moral means toward the goal of meeting all needs. Equity is applied to all aspects of the partnership, including very personal ones like receiving emotional support, for example, or really slowing down and listening to one's partner. The only question on the table is whether each partner's needs were met at any particular time. Delays might be inevitable, adjustments or even deferments might be necessary but if it is a partner's need then the aim is to fulfill it. The Unequal partners can be relied upon to check and re-check to be sure that the answer to need fulfillment is yes. Yes, indeed.

Who gets to say what is fair? Only the partners get to assess their needs. Only the partners get to say how they will address their needs. Their motivation is always their couple happiness. The individual focus is always on their partner's happiness as the highest priority. Unequal Partners expect to create personal happiness through their own efforts. They are the actors. They are the determiners of their happiness. This is radical thinking, to be sure. Unequal Partners refuse to leave their personal happiness to the ravages of romantic fantasy or the roll of the dice from their families' expectations or from society's cultural pressures. Not that Unequal Partners aren't influenced just like other people <u>but</u> having a commitment of making your partner your highest priority goes a long way toward aligning <u>who</u> and <u>what</u> you will allow to influence you and to what degree.

Unequal Partners want equity, not equality. Equity is the natural offspring of their commitment to each other's happiness. Any logical pursuit of their happiness must focus on the partners attempting to meet all needs. They don't care about equal portions of this and that. They are not counting to see how much their partner received of whatever. The partners are not keeping track of who did or did not do the laundry as a matter of fairness. Their thinking is "we have leading partner needs + implementing partner needs that we must try to meet as best we can." Whether the issue is handling their money and other assets or the issue is how to meet one of the partner's need for cuddling and to be listened to, either way, the partners will apportion the needed resources as best they can to make everybody happy.

As far as the laundry is concerned, the partners make agreements about how responsibilities are to be dealt with. Unequal Partners make their overall goal of attempting to meet all their needs in pursuit of their happiness as the basis for their decisions about who does laundry or, otherwise, how chores get done. Unequal Partners would not start with "the laundry needs to get done." If they did the <u>only</u> answer discussion and agreement would net them is who does the laundry (this time). The Unequal Partner way of life asks, "Who gets to be happy?" The answer is "we do (because we saw to it) AND the laundry got done (by one of us who likes doing laundry or both of us OR by arranging to have someone else do it)."

Leader, leading position, life partner, my partner, my lover, husband, wife, dominant: one of the partners holds special responsibility for the direction of the relationship and the integrity of the relationship as it evolves. The partnership is the responsibility of both partners, of course, but one of them takes an extra dose of responsibility where the larger picture is concerned. The leading partner is super-watchful of their metaphorical relationship container, which is composed of their agreements. The leading partner is monitoring

- The general health of the relationship
- The positioning of the relationship relative to the partners' agreed upon goals and
- The overall direction of the relationship (Where are we headed and why? What is our purpose?).

Who gets to be in lead position? What makes one of the partners the leader? The lead is discussed and agreed upon but is based on the leading partner's True Nature. The best person for that set of responsibilities takes the lead position. Each according to their True Nature.

Actually, "Who gets to be the leader?" might sound too much like "Who gets the privileged spot?" Allow me to try again for accuracy. The two positions, the leading one and the implementing one, have the same status. By their very nature one of the partners can more easily take on the meta-level of concern (big picture stuff) for the partnership's well-being. Think of that person's nature and/or personality as being well formed for this job. They make it look easy and it is easy for them because it is their nature. The leading partner is happy taking care of their family from their leading position. They get to shine as their fullest expression of who they really are. The implementing partner is proud of their leading partner's abilities and the other way around is also true.

Otherwise, where tasks must be organized and carried out partners will work in whatever work configuration that gets the job done and meets their needs. It could also be the case that one partner might take on the duties of the other for some length of time. What if one of you becomes ill or comes home exhausted? Organizing labor might take a flip, too, in light of the fact that one of you is the knowledge expert or most experienced for a particular task.

So, leading does not constitute giving orders while someone else provides the labor. Leading has to do with gentle, intelligent guidance of the family based on the leader's understanding of all needs. Leading is a gentle responsibility. It is kind and diplomatic. Leadership in the Unequal Partnership model uses, without exception, collaborative methods and inclusive decision-making.

Implementer, implementing position, life partner, husband, wife, submissive: one of the partners is supporting and implementing. The implementing partner picks up the ball for carrying out the two partners' decisions. This partner position as supporting and implementing is by agreement and is based on the implementing partner's True Nature. One of the partners can best express who they really are from the implementing position. They will be the happiest and that's what's important.

The implementing partner is an excellent follow-through person. The partners together constitute a team.[4] The team is continuously creating agreements. Somebody has to design plans that will get the family unit to their goals. Somebody has to keep everyone's eyes on the family's goals. Just like the leading partner, the implementing partner does not expect to think or act alone. Instead, the implementing partner acts in concert with his/her partner. The implementer, just like the leading partner, has strong involvement in the bigger issues such as determining shared values or the general direction of the relationship. At the same time the implementer is pledged to have the most focus on what it takes to meet their agreed upon goals.

The implementing partner delights in keeping schedules, watching the calendar, calling family meetings, and, perhaps, maintaining a planner. Things don't get forgotten or overlooked. Detail-oriented. That's our implementing partner.

The implementer might be the domestic in the family but not necessarily. He or she might be really good at wrangling family members to get all the domestic chores done cooperatively. The point is always getting things done. We have no need or desire to turn anyone in the family into the domestic mule. I had a relationship with a woman who loved caring for the domestic arena. That was her thing. She derived her sense of self from how well she cared for our home. In that case I was supporting her happiness by getting out of the way as she swept or put groceries away. My meta-responsibility for us was to keep us organized and to watch out for our larger goals as a couple, none of which was her talent. She appreciated my ability to hold it all together for us. I appreciated how well she made a home for us. I still dried dishes whenever I was at home and we enjoyed folding clothes together.

Here's another example: if the partners are agreed that one of their goals is to vacation in London next summer then we'd expect the implementing partner to take the lead responsibility for researching what would be needed for their trip. They might call a family meeting to discuss finances. Savings plan, anyone? In yet another example, the leading partner may take great pleasure in cooking family meals. Terrific. He cooks. She does the shopping because she actually likes being in stores. Maybe this couple loves doing the dishes together. Or, everybody hates washing dishes so-o-o the dishwasher is an important labor saving device in their home.

Implementers are usually highly intelligent get-things-done types. They stay busy but they stay organized as well. They know where they are going and what to do when they get there. Implementers are usually kind and patient and eager to please. Expect an implementer to have lots of skills and talents. They just need their leading partner to whom they can pledge their lifelong loyalty. Leading partners show great appreciation for their implementing partners.

If an implementing type person dates a leading personality and they continue forward with that person then they are at least implicitly agreeing to be related to as the opposite of a dominant/leading personality. I, leading partner. You, implementing partner.

Obviously, language is important. I, the author, am reticent to use the word "supporting" because it might imply "little helper" in some readers' minds. There is nothing diminutive about the implementing position, for starters. Secondly, "helper" suggests that one of you is support services for someone else's project or vision for life. Yes, of course, there are implementers out there who are perfectly happy with the notion that they are giving support services. They see themselves as devoted to their leading partner's guidance for their lives. Fine. Wonderful. I have met many of these couples. Others would prefer to describe themselves as part of a collaborative team with each partner having a different set of responsibilities and focus. A difference of focus or emphasis in responsibilities marks the difference between the two positions, instead of status. In either rendering the implementer is not passive. They are an agent in their own right. The implementing partner is an active determining factor in the Unequal Partnership.

I see "supporting" as a gentle art inside an intimate relationship on both sides. But "supporting" might become associated with the implementation side because the implementing partner takes comparatively more responsibility for the follow through on the couple's decision making. Here, the images of a ship, the captain of the ship, and the first mate might be helpful to some of you. Go with what feels right for you.

Now, let's talk about that word "submissive." It's a positive term from the BDSM world. There are "submissive" personalities. They have a range of desire to be in the service of a dominant/leading partner. Some want to be in a relationship with a dominant, for sure, but without that relationship they still have a sense of themselves as being submissive. Others need to be with a dominant/leader for the sub self to be activated. Self-actualization happens but only within a committed relationship. That is to say that these people are more alive—more themselves--when they find their dominant life partner (dom, domme, mistress, master, owner, and other meaningful names).

Neither submissive is without voice or self-determination. They have tremendous integrity along with their loyalty and devotion to their dominant. Each and every submissive that I know well is a strong personality. They are usually dominant in their work lives and highly successful. In their personal lives they choose to be on the other side of dominance. They wish to be of service. Some hold their acts of service to be sacred.

I'd like it to be known that thousands of people want a non-egalitarian model for their relationship but specifically do not want to be identified with kink. Hurray. Wonderful to be kinky if that's your thing but if it's not then that's okay, too. You are in luck. The Unequal Partnership is based on hierarchy but not traditional ideas of equality. This base as I have explained it here holds up well with or without kink. The couple makes an agreement that power and control will slant toward one of them. This is a conscious choice that feels great. It gives the leading partner the ability 1. To create a synthesis of all needs at any time and 2. To use that synthesis to form decisions for the good of the whole and 3. It gives the implementing partner freedom to focus on the meaty everyday concerns that advance the objectives and goals of the couple. You can call yourself whatever you want. I've given you lots of suggestions that have nothing to do with kink from many real life Unequal Partnership couples:

---Leader, my leading partner, husband, wife, my life partner, my partner, my lover and

---Implementer, my implementing partner, my life partner, my partner, husband, wife, my lover.

The only essential factor is that the couple knowingly slants power and control in the relationship dynamic for the purpose of best pursuing their individual and collective personal happiness. Each partner is empowered by these conditions. Otherwise, it's not the creation of an Unequal Partnership. It's something else.

Partnership: an Unequal Partnership arrangement is a partnership. Being partners is way cooler than being mere romantic lovers. Partners have powers. They place their obligations and responsibilities above all else; therefore, romance and love are well supported. They feel free to be romantic. Their relationship business is taken care of all the time. Romance can flourish. Still, not everyone likes the term "partner" in reference to his or her Romantic

Others. Too much like "business partner," right? Perhaps, in some minds, it suggests emotional distance as with a business partner. I can see that. I agree. I agree that "partnering" is being borrowed from a business context to be applied to an intimate environment. I'd like to be clear that, yes, there is plenty of business seriousness in navigating an Unequal Partnership. It is your business to set up conditions that will take care of you both regardless of what relationship mode that you adopt. The intimate partnership's conditions are, of course, constantly changing or, we can say, are in a continuous state of creation. Unequal partners expect change and expect to negotiate and re-negotiate. They expect to always be re-evaluating what's needed and whether their collective needs are being met. The hard work of partnering is the very serious business that makes sticking together for a lifetime possible if that's what you want.

Unequal Partnership couples negotiate like crazy and keep a tight watch on how their partner is faring. They have an expectation of closeness with their partner maintained by strong communication. The partners make and keep agreements as normal business between them. They are immensely respectful and kind toward each other even when tired or angry or uncomfortable. All of this amounts to deliberate contractual partnering. Does that sound serious? I hope that it does. It's the business of building and maintaining a stable long-term loving relationship the Unequal Partnership way. If you do your business right--the business of Unequal Partnership—then the rewards are things like stability, personal satisfaction, and romance, lots of passionate romance.

Giving up fear for the reward of partnership. Each person, new to leading or implementing, approaches the other person with Boyfriend/girlfriend mentality in their every cell 'cuz it's what we know. To form an Unequal Partnership each must drop worrying about whether his/her needs will get met. The Boyfriend/girlfriend scenario teaches us that there is no one to look out for my needs except me even when I am in an intimate, steadfast relationship. Ultimately, only I am going to represent and advocate for my needs. Whatever support I receive from my lover is a bonus. That's just the way it is. But what if I gave up such a worry? What might happen? I can hear you gasp at the prospect. What terrible thing might happen to me? Well, my needs just wouldn't get met and it would be my fault---no one else's.[5]

Many, if not most, Americans associate individualism, self-reliance, independence, and "not giving away too much" as just good common sense even in what's intended to be a deep love relationship. "But I don't want to lose myself in the relationship. I'm still responsible for me. With the wrong kind of attitude I might wake up one day and not know who I am." Really? Does that happen? I have had old married couples who've told me that this is so. They say that it is possible for someone to lose all sense of himself/herself in a relationship. I say, not in a healthy relationship. I can tell you that a true partner would never ask to obliterate your personality in the service of their needs. Never. Quite the reverse. The partner honors who you are and wants even more of you to show up in the relationship. "What do you want and how do you wish to grow further?" That's what a partner constantly has on their mind. "I don't want to lose my independence," says the Boyfriend/girlfriend scenario. A partner does not want you to lose your independence or whatever makes you You. Partnership requires two independent thinkers, that is, two mature adults. There probably is a boyfriend out there who might like the idea of seeing you succumb to his needs and wants to direct your life from there. But a real friend—boy or girl--would not have such a nefarious agenda. By contrast, someone who wants the best for you as their first priority is someone to take seriously in your life. They just might be someone to consider as a prospective partner.

Partnership requires letting go of fear. In the Unequal Partnership case it's the fear of not getting your needs met that must be faced. Hardly any of us can help but enter an intimate relationship quivering a bit or a lot because we are scared that, among other things, we don't know the particulars about how our needs are going to get met. You know that one and you can do something other than dump on your new life partner. Now, if you would, please, take a long slow breath. Yes, right now, as you are reading this. Take a minute to imagine real trust. Warm, just-right trust streaming into your senses at your invitation at just the right pace. That's the replacement for all that uncertainty you were taught to expect in a relationship. It's called trust. You're going to give it to your partner and you're going to expect to receive it. Over time and with real life experiences, you'll build trust in your partner to take care of your needs. But for now let's get back to dating reality: over your dating experiences trust deepens to this extraordinary level of partnership or it does not. So, keep as eye out.

The Unequal Partnership model asks each person to switch their focus to their partner's needs. You give up worrying about whether your needs will get met and, instead, focus on your partner's needs. The partner does the same. The partners say to each other, "I promise to hold your needs as paramount and as the first in my considerations." Worrying about whether your needs will get met = distrust and fear = lack of closeness with your prospective loved one. Is that what you want?

In the Unequal Partnership trust fills in the void where once there was fear and holds each partner more substantially than the distrust and suspicion that rides along with worry about whether your needs are going to get met. Trust. The partners collapse forward into a delicious, yummy lean on each other. I call this **The Lean In**. It's neither co-dependence nor dependence. It's interdependence. It's priceless and healthy. There is no burden here. There will be extremely little strife inside such a relationship. There are the solid beginnings of a lifetime structure for the partners: "I've got you." "I've got you, too."

The Unequal Partnership model has two metaphors that explain a lot. I think you'll find them both enlightening and romantic:

Partnership as metaphor: the Boyfriend/girl-friend scenario tells us that there is love, romance, and a relationship that will never end waiting for you. But why are we motivated to follow that cultural norm? It seems that everybody is doing it. An extremely high American divorce rate does not discourage people from following the only romance behaviors that Americans know.[6] I would argue that every couple following the Boyfriend/girlfriend thing hopes and prays for a better outcome for themselves: "Forget about the high divorce rate. We love each other so much. We will be different. We will beat the odds."

All humans crave a deep emotional connection. We, humans, have a primal instinct that drives us toward each other and not just romantically. We want a profound emotional experience. Well, okay, then. The boyfriend/girlfriend scenario requires commitment to limiting emotional risk for the sake of individualism and a false sense of individual security. Think about that. It's not exactly what each of us is consciously saying to ourselves but the programming is there. That's a built in

Boyfriend/girlfriend limiter on closeness. It's not that Boyfriend/girlfriend couples don't form to great success but the odds are unfavorable for endurance and certainly against forming partnership. The Unequal Partnership model requires emotional high risk in order to reach the goal of deep emotional connection. As I've said, Unequal Partnership is not for everyone.

We have already talked about hierarchy as opposed to practicing egalitarianism. Now, here we are at the next big issue that might not be attractive to some ---emotional high risk. For those who have gone that far it is a state of being that is sweet. Sweet, for sure. I can explain how Unequal Partnership achieves and maintains deep emotional connection. I'll tell you a story. In fact, you can help tell it:

Raise your open hands and turn them so that your palms are facing each other. Your hands represent two dating persons. Move your hands closer and closer to represent dating going well. In the Boyfriend/girlfriend scenario romantically successful couples almost touch or barely touch. Their success looks like being able to maintain good communication and good but limited sharing of personal desires and feelings. So, at the best, a

Boyfriend/girlfriend type couple's good communication meets the base requirement for sustainability. They share regularly and, therefore, hold each other closely. They have a good chance at long-term sustainability as long as they maintain good communication and as long as sharing of personal needs and desires has some depth. Most couples within the Boyfriend/girlfriend schema are not seeking this level of closeness. Too risky. Too much bother and work to support the other person's desires, not your own, not your own directly, that is.

Pull your hands apart again. Begin to move your hands closer and closer. This time it's an Unequal Partnership couple that's dating. Move the hands closer still. When your hands are just touching, pause. This is the couple having gotten to know each other well and is now ready to commit. Commitment looks like letting go of the fear that your needs might not get met. Commitment looks like letting go of the idea that you have to remain the absolute defender of your needs.

This uncommon remarkable phenomenon of giving up fear in the presence of the beloved has happened gradually, of course. The day comes though when fear is *released in the presence of the new beloved. Over your dating history you would have each had actual experiences of releasing responsibility for getting your needs met and realizing that your prospective partner was right there to pick up that responsibility. You did not have to trust words, instead real and satisfying experiences repeatedly gave you reason to trust beyond what's usual. The space that fear energy once held is filled by trust. Your beloved has done the same. Allow your fingers to interlace. This is the Unequal Partnership's **Lean In**. Trust with a capital "T" causes **The Lean In**. You and your new partner trust each other in a deep way. You are dependent on each other in a positive healthy way. It feels fantastic. Once there, you'll fight off anything the world throws at you, two, that might threaten your deep connection.*

As for internal discord, imagine the Unequal Partnership couple having an argument or one of you is unhappy about something. One hand tries to pull away from the interlacing fingers. Somebody is full up with emotion. Okay. It happens. Before the partnership can get back on track, you, the other partner, must move with your partner! One hand moves to join the hand that tried to pull away. Get closer when there is an imbalance.

Look at the beloved. See the beloved whom you must move toward. Only by moving to where she is will you know how she is feeling. You'll know the emotion. By doing so you'll raise the trust level between you at a vulnerable time. Staying close to the partner builds assurance that you are there for each other. Only then can you move back on the path. Now, you're moving again. You're moving because you're able to do so. You'll move together as a true partnership. You'll feel great. What a relationship success. What happiness.

The Daily Mechanics of Relationship as Metaphor: Relationships have structure. Most, not all, intimate relationships are a free-for-all with next to nothing in deliberate structuring. A new relationship will eventually settle into some kind of shaping forged from implicit and some explicit understandings about who holds power in the relationship, behavioral patterns, personal preferences, and their needs as a couple.

In the Unequal Partnership case, structure for the couple's relationship is purposefully, deliberately designed to fit their needs. And as their needs change the couple isn't hesitant to renegotiate. Such a couple is laying down the foundation that governs their behavior and interactions between them. That structure holds them as they interact daily and always. Structure gives them a unique container that they can count on. As Life happens their relationship structure gives them direction, gives them answers about behavior between them, and answers about their behavior as a couple interacting with the world. It reminds them clearly of who they are because their foundation was made by their agreements and the truth of who they say that they are.

The Unequal Partnership arrangement in total can be thought of as having a shell or container with a soft creamy romantic center that is the constant fluid interactions of the couple. The Unequal Partnership has negotiation or shared understandings resulting from excellent communication. The Unequal Partnership has an outer container (their agreements) plus the couple's interactions happening inside their relationship container. Think about structure as a product of the couple's negotiated agreements (for rules and for the parameters of acceptable behavior), so, of course, their relationship container is malleable. Day-to-day couple interactions--the soft creamy romantic center--re-create structure continuously. Unequal Partnership has deliberate structure continuously created and recreated by the partners themselves. The target of Unequal relationship structure is the couple's personal happiness.

Let's review:

Leading partners are concerned with all aspects of the relationship but emphasize or have a particular focus on the structural health, on-going and long term, of the relationship and

Implementing partners are concerned with all aspects of the relationship but have a particular focus on the implementation of the couple's decision making in day-to-day life and more.

Boyfriend/girlfriend scenario

1. Love is enough to deal with life together,

2. Ultimately, I can only rely on myself to see that my needs are met, and

3. Fear and distrust are typical instead of unusual.

Unequal Partnership

      a. Love + taking care of relationship business = best chance at long term sustainable relationship,

      b. The trust metaphor is at the romantic core of an Unequal Partnership: trust causes partners to **Lean In** and interdepend to an extraordinary degree,

      c. The relationship metaphor for the Unequal Partnership is **The Container** that the partners create and re-create via their agreements. It creates a foundation for the couple, one that they can rely on when Life brings them uncomfortable or difficult situations.

      d. Unequal Partners are their own activists for continuous love and trust.

Chapter Two:
Power and Control in a Relationship
Or What to Look Out for as You Date

This chapter contains my best talk on what to look out for as you attempt to find your Unequal Partner. You want

      1. Power With, not Power Over with the person that you are dating,

      2. A situation of empowerment for yourself as opposed to a subjugation of self. You should feel as though you are bigger and better when you are with this person, not smaller and less than,

      3. To be secure enough in your own being that you are never a Taker,

      4. To avoid manipulation and power grabs, and

      5. To be always headed toward negotiations.

Power and control exist in human interactions that are as simple as a friendly conversation between two strangers. Even before a chat begins between strangers the two have sized each other up based on clothing, body language, any extras like an expensive briefcase or a fancy car, language and regional dialect, hairstyle, eye contact or the lack thereof, attitude and energy. The viewer's previous experiences and cultural expectations filter all of that. Romantic sizing up happens in just this way, as well.

Consider relationships that you think that you have some knowledge of. Think back to the relationships that you witnessed as a child: that of your parents and their friends, of your relatives, of your teachers and their spouses. There was power there and you knew it. You knew. Studies show that where the power between mother and father is greatly favoring one parent over the other, the children grow up with a love/hate for the lower ranking parent since survival forces them to identify more strongly with the power grabber.[7] That's one consequence of what happens in a One Down/Power Taking dynamic. Daughters of narcissistic mothers, for example, of which there are millions, grew up with a mom who was self-absorbed and unable to love but who held all the power in the family. The negative effects on the adult daughter's life are extremely harmful and lasting.[8]

Very differently, during your childhood, did you witness or really get to experience a romantic relationship between equals? Not a lot of those in effect even though popular culture and common belief holds that most romantic relationships are an equal contract. Think deeply about this one. When have you ever experienced a relationship of equals?

Seriously consider, in the relationships that you are currently aware of, where the power lies. Who has the most control over anything and, maybe, everything in that relationship? Perhaps one person manipulates the other into getting their way or uses various methods of intimidation to control the other. Or, there may exist a tacit agreement of being the one who controls the relationship without democratic decision-making. Who can really make their presence felt in the relationship and how do they do it? In answering any one or all of these questions you are focusing on power in intimate relationships from your own experience. Power. Control. You do know.

Power. Control. These are the reflexive muscles in a relationship. It is reflexive because orientation toward power and control comes from a deep place in the psyche. Your own orientation depends on both nature and nurture. You were born with certain personality traits and tendencies. You, the newborn, already had a certain temperament that your parents quickly discovered as you showed them how easily you rolled into being a new person in the world or maybe you showed them the exact opposite. But how you respond as a child and later as an adult in relation to power and control is also strongly influenced by your home and school environments. Lots of scholarly and popular culture literature on these subjects.[9]

1. Power with, not power over

We, all, know examples from our own lives or, perhaps, only from the newspapers, of power in the domineering, controlling sense. Have you experienced the will of a person who did not mean well by you but claimed to have your best interest in mind? Too many of us have been at the mercy of a controlling personality determined to dictate reality to us. I have spent a lot of therapy hours on this because of my narcissistic mother and then because of the man that I married. Such a situation can introduce a range of experiences from annoyance to feeling abused. Keep in mind that abuse is not always physical. Emotional/psychological is just as damaging. Conversely, too many of us are that controlling, obnoxious, domineering person who needs to have a person that they can run ragged and drive crazy. If that's you, please, raise your hand.

An Unequal Partnership has shared power between the two partners. No leading partner has any desire or will to dominate, as in take advantage of, his or her partner or anyone else. Leading partners as described here tend to be nurturers who feel a great deal of responsibility for their family's well-being. The implementing partner is far from a pushover looking to be dominated. The two partners use their different roles to allocate their labor and energy across necessary responsibilities and duties. They keep the needs of their partner first in their minds.

The Implementing partner speaks to his/her needs, contributes his opinions at will, pays attention to the health and happiness of the partner, and just like the leading partner he or she works independently to carry out the agreed upon tasks in order to meet agreed upon goals.

Both leading partner and implementing partner are trusted, mature adults working toward the good of the relationship. We refer to their mutual trust plus the execution of their individual set of responsibilities in concert with their partner as a Power With arrangement.

Power Over would look like micromanaging, harassing, possibly belittling, and other strategies aimed at controlling the other person's behavior. A controlling personality isn't likely to be introspective and self-correcting. Because of their controlling nature they are unlikely to consider contrasting points of view. The domineering personality is unlikely to really listen to their partner. This out of control personality will not show continuous respect for the partner by taking the partner's opinions and needs seriously. Make sure that you are spending your precious time with someone who feels secure in himself/herself and, therefore, has no need or desire to try to control you. Unequal Partnership leaders manage or give guidance to the direction and overall health of the relationship. What the leading partner offers is an act of service. It's an important distinction that the leading partner has no desire or compulsion to control someone's behavior.

Power Over does not fulfill the tenets of an Unequal Partnership. Controlling behavior can be expected to interfere with a person's freedom to behave naturally at home. Controlling behavior can be expected to destroy trust between the two.

A Power Over arrangement is always a set of implicit agreements that the two parties slid into. No one ever explicitly signs over his or her rights to a bully.

Power With is all about sharing and jointly holding the weight of responsibilities of the relationship. Power With in an Unequal Partnership relationship is all about respecting each other's needs. When the leading partner speaks the implementing partner listens and cares. When the implementing partner speaks the leading partner listens and cares. The decision making of the Unequal couple is inclusive and ultimately reflects the needs of both partners.

2. Subjugation of self is anathema to an Unequal Partnership.

In the Power Over scenario a domineering person bullies someone into expressing <u>less</u> of himself/herself. Remember that bullying isn't always obvious. It could be that over time one person finds himself with less and less energy or power to even try to assert his wants and needs at home. It just seems easier to let the other person have his or her way. Not only does the bullied person have less say in decision-making but more than that they have a smaller personality footprint overall in the relationship. There is less of who they are being expressed. Period. Less and less of that bullied person's character is showing up in what might have once been a partnership. There is no partnership. The bullied person's Deepest Self becomes practiced at staying quiet. The bullied person has little voice or none at all. No partnering going on here.

Now, switch and think about the domineering person. That person isn't sharing their Deepest Self either and isn't any more present in the relationship than the bullied partner even though it seems as though that person is omnipresent or too present. The domineering person takes up a lot of space energetically but that fact is not the same as sharing themselves. That spewing out of energy is out of control behavior. It has the single purpose of hogging attention instead of being loving. Loving and caring for the other person is not paramount in a bully's thinking no matter what they are telling themselves. I believe that the person on either side of an abusive dynamic is starved for emotional connection. Neither person is fully present in the relationship so how can there be meaningful connection? There can be no deep emotional connection in this sort of power dynamic. An Unequal Partnership has a goal of creating and maintaining conditions for deep emotional connection.

If either partner believes that service to others means denying their own needs they are strongly mistaken. Keeping yourself tucked inside as though you have no needs is also a misconception of what it means to partner or to be of service.

Assuming that a partnership began at all, the manifestation of any or some of the traits discussed here is the death of partnership. By strong contrast, you and your future partner can stand tall as an Unequal Partnership couple. What could be more empowering than a relationship that by its contractual nature requires you to bring all of you, all aspects of self, to the table and then to grow further and be more?

3. Take versus Receiving (It's a Gift)

There is a terrible misconception of leadership loose in the world--the leader dictates or commands and the follower follows. Maybe that is true in a military model but it is far from the realities of Unequal Partnership. Leading partners do not <u>take</u> from their loved ones. Their personalities are such that the urge to be a Taker isn't there. They feel the very opposite. They are generous to a fault. Leading partners are, also, sensitive to the loving support they receive from their loved one. They tend to be gracious in the receiving.

Implementing partners are not takers. They are not scheming to get their needs met. The implementing partner has faith and trust in their partner's ability to care for them through excellent communication plus good decision-making. Implementing partners tend to be gracious receivers, too. Faith and trust are gifts from both sides. Support in a relationship given by either partner is a gift of love.

4. Things to Avoid

Avoid dating someone who is an unknown. Vet your prospective leading or implementing partner. Ask the person you are dating for references and check them. If they balk then consider their absence in your life as no loss.

Avoid the Shutdown Artist. This is the person who is

very good at shutting down discussion. They are not open and affirming. They do not value difference of opinion. They do not appreciate discovering more about you. They will not honor who you are. Their tactic for shutting down discussion can be talking too loudly or changing the subject. It can be giving their attention to their smartphone instead of listening to you.

Avoid the slanting of power and control that doesn't feel good to you. The prospective partners should be able to talk explicitly about control in the relationship. As you are dating make sure that you are speaking clearly about your own needs; do not expect mind reading. Instead, expect that you, two, are forming a slanting of power and control together. If this is not the case then this is not a good situation for you. Ask yourself: "am I giving up some control because I want to do so or do I feel pushed, shoved, gently or otherwise manipulated, coerced maybe? Are things moving along comfortably or do I feel rushed?"

Avoid ignoring your intuitive knowledge. Use your intuition to stay safe. It's a natural alarm system. Listen to it and ACT. If a situation feels good and you feel empowered then go forward if you want. If your gut is gripping tight even a little then HOLD UP. Notice if your date is persistent in trying to see to your needs. Maybe they were at first but now not so much? Your right person consistently will show you kindness, respect, and support. If things are questionable now during dating don't think that they will improve once you, two, commit. Don't make excuses for the other person's behavior.

Avoid becoming isolated. You may have started out with lots of friends but now find yourself in a tiny world of two, controlled by a dominant. If some level of strict control makes you happy then good for you both. You got what you wanted. But if not, don't feel stuck. Initial consent is not final. Repeatedly review whether you have what you want. Are you happy? Isolation of the prospective leading partner can happen, too. Imagine that you find yourself with a particularly passive-aggressive prospective implementing partner who whines and complains whenever you propose visiting your relatives.

Avoid manipulation and power grabs. Yes, manipulation can happen on either side. At the first signs of it you have serious decisions to make about whether you are going forward. As for power grabs from the implementer side, watch out for struggles over control. If there is a pattern then you are left having to assess whether this is really your person or not.

Avoid the prospective partner who demonstrates a great introductory package but soon seems to have run out of energy and/or has totally lost focus. You are going to need a real partner so look for a tenacious nature in the person you are dating. Your right person consistently will show you kindness, respect, and support as your dating history accumulates. You should see an ability to stick to it as situations arise.

Avoid using people as objects. Anyone wanting a successful dating result should take a high interest in their date's wants and needs. Avoid using people just as a means to get what you want. By concentrating on your dating partner's needs you are more likely to find the pleasure and satisfaction you seek for yourself.

Unequal Partnership, a non-egalitarian model requires strong partnering skills. Behaving like a partner even in a light sense during dating can only set a solid footing toward a stable, long-term relationship.

As your dating experiences accumulate you'll come to realize that a partnership was forming. It will have seemed effortless and that is what you want. Nobody is using anybody.

5. Always be Headed toward Negotiations

While you are dating you are sounding out how each of you feels about many issues. If you get to the point of considering this person seriously then the leading partner should be steering the two of you toward formal negotiations. Some people like relationship contracts, a non-legal document that sets down your agreements. If you, two, want a contract then write down your most important agreements and make the contract time-limited. With or without a contract, your joint intention is to meet all needs. Maintain an attitude that you can and will negotiate again and again as needed.

Chapter 8 will explore partner negotiation. It's really important to learn to negotiate with a goal of meeting your needs as a couple.

Chapter Three:
Now, Let's Do Some Dating.
First, check yourself.

Two things for introspection:

      1. What do you bring to the table for an Unequal Partnership?

      2. Do you know what you want? Get clear.

What would <u>you</u> bring to an Unequal Partnership?

I wrote this book for people who want so much more than the Boyfriend/girlfriend relationship scenario. You are my kind of person if you are already thinking about what kind of relationship that you want, thinking about what kind of person might partner well with you, and, last, if you are thinking about what <u>you</u> bring to the potential relationship. Let's start with that last point and work our way toward what is on your wish list for a partnership.

Are you preparing for the loving relationship that you want? If it were handed to you tomorrow would you be

ready? We, all, have something to improve upon but don't
be like a guy in my past who never bothered to clip nose
hairs, even after I gently told him that I really couldn't stand
to look at those. He also had fuzzy hairs on his earlobes. He
just didn't care except when I said something. His attitude
was not consistent with partnering. The guy had no lasting
energy as a partner and definitely did not make my needs
first. I could continue with what you should not do but
instead let's take a positive turn so that you (and I) can stop
thinking about nose hairs.

You want a sweet and wonderful partnership that has
the bones to last a very long time. Those do not grow on
banana trees. You must work on what you want everyday
beginning with adjusting your attitude as needed. Many life
coaches and inspirational speakers have asked audiences or
church congregations to think through the week about where
their minds live, mostly in positive or mostly in negative
thinking. Furthermore, one congregation was asked to
notice how long they could go without a negative thought
imposing itself on one's day. It might be a useful exercise for
a dating person who hopes to one day live with, laugh with,
work with, face Life's bumps and sorrows with another
person. You know what I'm saying here. Isn't it worth it to

put some real effort into achieving your goal of a loving sustainable relationship right now? Today?

Do you have time in your life for a relationship? This one sometimes trips up males. They were so focused on pursuing a relationship that it never occurred to them that their life was already full up. No space in a busy life. Well, you might say, such a person—male or female--can make change, shift things around, and give something up after the right person shows up. How about having these conversations with yourself now in the dating phase? What will it mean to spend significant time with your new loved one? What's very important to you and you wish to continue even after you are coupled? Be honest with yourself. Be honest with your prospective partner.

Are there people who don't belong in your life for whatever reason? Are you ready to let those Hangers On go? Who is in your life in a positive way? Who might lend support to your new relationship? Who do you feel closest to?

How are you very much like your parents? How are you very different? What might you want in your partnership that's very different from your parents' lifestyle?

What kind of work do you do? Is it career-oriented? Whether it is or not, are you happy work-wise? What would you change if you could? Long-term goals?

What are your current life goals? What are your plans for now? Long-term goals?

How do you usually handle disagreements? How do you feel about deciding small matters like where to go for dinner? How might you handle larger issues like saving for retirement if you had your Unequal partner today?

How able are you to speak about your needs and speak up for your needs? How good are you about listening to and respecting someone else's needs?

What Do You Have to Offer? Ideas about Implementer Skills:

You may have lovely talents like the ability to sing, to play an instrument, or to write poetry or online blogs. Perhaps, you are a terrific public speaker. Maybe, you are college-educated or highly skilled. Are you a professional chef or a wonderful home cook? Really great organizational skills? How developed are your soft skills such as being a really good listener, having patience, being observant, having or developing tenacity, or having lots of positive relationship energy to offer. How about having an intention to grow further? It's a good idea to work on being a clear communicator. How easily can you speak about your own needs?

What Do You Have to Offer? Ideas about Leading Partner Skills:

You can check out your Unequal leadership muscles by reading business leadership classics like Whale Done by Kenneth Blanchard. Leading partners take responsibility for the structural elements of the relationship. Expect to have the most focus on big picture items like the direction of the relationship. Look for good resources to support you. Read a lot. Find a good mentor if you are new to taking leadership in a relationship.

Be prepared to articulate your understanding of the relationship that you want. Be ready to answer questions about how you would like to proceed. Be flexible in your thinking. Practice inclusive decision-making now while you are still dating so that you and your prospective partner can begin to act as an effective team.

How interesting a person are you? Are you comparing yourself to other people, or, perhaps, well-known characters in popular culture? Please stop. In order to get ready for partnership you must do your assessments by comparing you to you. Are you growing? Is that even a question in your life? Are you learning new things? I know individuals who aren't taking in much information from their environment. Some people are not scintillating conversationalist but what's notable is that they are not working on improving. Others know well that they do not care about people and community and yet they want a mate for themselves. I know people who haven't thought about trees and earth and little animals and the rest of Nature in years. How awake and vibrant are you?

To be a good partner, leading or implementing, you will need

- Kindness and patience,

- A generally positive outlook on life,

- A good measure of self-awareness and self-acceptance,

- The ability and will to pay attention,

- An exploring nature (I want to know you, my partner, and I accept that our everyday with each other is yet another day of discovery),

- An exploring nature in the sense that you are open to learning and acquiring new knowledge,

- A loving nature,

- Tenacity,

- To be a good listener,

- Resilience and flexibility in the face of hard times and flexibility,

- Honesty,

- A sense of being part of a larger living scheme such as family, community, part of the Earth, part of a living Universe.

- Leaders have a big dose of meta-level (the big picture) thinking, which does not cost them pain or discomfort. It's all in their nature.

- Implementers have a natural ability to deal with lots of threads at once and a strong follow through sense. Some people can deal with life's occasional madness without the situation becoming maddening for them.

Let's examine that list in slo-mo:

• Kindness and patience. This one speaks for itself except that I would say that it includes having a generally positive attitude toward life. You are a well-developed person who is pleasant---even, fun---to be around. You exhibit kindness toward others; you wouldn't think of doing otherwise.

• A good measure of self-awareness and self-acceptance. Let's hear a big, loud Ta-da for self-love. Are you keeping up your appearance because you like looking good, smelling fresh, and adore your own dewy soft skin? I hope so. Are you actively working on having good conversation skills? I see characters in the movies that have no social game. Funny to laugh at, right? Not so funny in real life. How about finding a class and working on developing terrific social skills? Those of us who are pretty good can always think about how well we are keeping up our highly desirable social abilities. I hope that your self-confidence is way up in the clouds. Exuding self-love and confidence is very sexy and attractive. In your head and in your heart and through your actions be the wonderful leading partner or implementing partner that a special someone would love to find. Do it. Be it today.

• Pays attention. Partners pay attention. I've had a few really good boyfriends whose goodness was in part marked by their willingness to pay attention to my needs. They did not go on to become life partners but that's a different story. Paying attention does not in itself turn a good boyfriend/girlfriend into a life partner but a life partner in a long term sustainable relationship must be great at paying attention. Neither leader nor the implementing partner can afford to shut down in this respect. There is no space in a healthy relationship for sleeping on the job. The first job of an excellent partner is paying attention. Pay attention to how your partner is feeling, how well they are faring in a difficult job situation, how much fatigue they might be feeling and what resources they have for replenishing themselves. Paying attention is the only way to move efficiently toward your goals, toward relationship goals, and all others.

• An exploring nature within the relationship. "I want to know you, my partner, and it pleases me that our everyday with each other is yet another day of discovery." Sounds like closeness to me.

• An exploring nature in the sense that you are open to learning and acquiring new knowledge. This trait does not require that you have several degrees but rather that you have intellectual curiosity. A recent prospective of mine showed little curiosity about what other people were doing or what they were creating or much else that was beyond his comfort zone. But then there was my father who had few opportunities to receive much formal education and yet that never stopped him from having a strong desire for learning and acquiring new knowledge. Being open to receiving new knowledge might include being open to attending workshops or classes that will give you new skills for the good health of the partnership. You must think about how to keep you, the leader, or you, the implementing partner healthy and growing all the time in order to give the partnership the best possible you. I had a boyfriend in the past that gave me much care and understanding and sweetness at first but sat passively in every sense eventually. He said that he had done all that was required to win me and to get our relationship started and now he could sit back. That might be some persons' view of how to be a good boyfriend but it leaves out so very much if what you are wanting to build is a partnership.

• To be a good listener. You'd think that this would be simple. It is for some people. I am not a fan of those who tell themselves that they are good listeners but cannot stop interrupting others and/or have a persistent focus on themselves and the next thing that they want to say. They are <u>not</u> listening. They are taking in very little information from the world around them. Improved listening skills are in order. I have coached my clients in this area. How else can you become a leader who stays on top of the needs of your family? You may imagine that you know the needs but without deep listening (which does not include your ego getting in the way) then you cannot truly hear what your partner is expressing.

• Resilience and flexibility in the face of hard times are always a blessing. Resilience: it's the ability to bounce back when things get tough. I have seen this in many couples. The good news is that if resilience isn't one of your strengths now you can learn a new pattern of resilience maybe from your life partner. Modern science says that some people have brains that lean that way. Well, good. It would be a tremendous boon if your leading partner or implementing partner were resilient. From either side of partnerships the pull to get up and build yourselves anew. After a flood damaged your home or illness ravaged not only health but also your bank accounts taking an attitude of resilience would be invaluable. Resilience is a wonderful trait to have been born with but don't worry. Resilience like many human characteristics can be practiced and attained. Teach the brain a new ability. If either of you seem to have it or only one of you bears it then I hope that you can see that resilience would be an excellent partnership skill to practice. Begin with positive thoughts about how things can be.

• Honesty. If you have ever heard one of my presentations you might have picked up on my definition of honesty in partnership. It definitely is not the dictionary definition but instead goes beyond it. Honesty refers to one's willingness to be revealing of self. Please, for the good health of your prospective partnership imagine building a relationship in which you are able to "speak your mind" as long as you are kind and respectful toward your partner. In partnership you and (s)he will create conditions in which you both feel safe exploring some deep desires and needs that probably have never been voiced before. In partnership you feel encouraged to grow and change. It's expected that you are going to change over the years together. Sometime in the future you are going to feel safe saying, "I seem to have these new interests. I don't know what to do with these ideas yet. I hope that we can talk about them." I have large numbers of clients, mostly male, who tell me that they wouldn't dare go home and tell their wives what they just told me, the counselor. It's always some deeply held desire or idea or something about their self-image. They are not feeling safe enough in the relationship to be revealing of self. Here's yet another thought for you to consider before you begin a relationship: Will you do your very best to be there as a kind and welcoming partner when your beloved needs exploratory conversations? This is what emotional intimacy looks like and I congratulate you both in advance.

• A sense of being part of a larger living scheme such as family, community, part of the Earth, part of a living Universe. Avoid connecting with someone who has no general interest in the world and in other people. I have dated males and females who seemed loving and caring at first but on close inspection their appearance as such was just emotional bait waved under my nose. They wanted a companion for themselves. That's all. This situation is very much the case of using other people as things that will fulfill certain needs of theirs. If someone says, "I love her" but then that same person is quite willing to ignore their neighbor or fails to help others as opportunities arise then they are not a loving person but rather they are practicing <u>need fulfillment</u>. Proscribing such a small world for themselves does harm to all involved in the end. I am a tremendous fan of people who practice empathy, compassion and generosity of heart.

Practice honest and clear communication skills. Dating will present you with plenty of opportunities to practice good clear communication. It should be second nature or a practiced skill or both no matter to whom you are speaking. This is a very valuable ability. You have so many reasons to use that ability while dating. Negotiating is going to come up and you are going to need your best abilities as a clear communicator. An author once encouraged readers to seize everyday opportunities to practice public speaking. This is a great strategy for improvement as a clear communicator. I know for sure that everyday life, including dating, presents opportunities to practice your ability to speak about yourself, to speak up for your needs, and to negotiate with others. Do it. Recognize a negotiation opportunity and go with it without hesitation. Congratulate yourself later for a job well done without regard for how things went.

> Practice. Here is your mini tutorial for clear communication. Make sure that you are able to utter the following as needed:
>
> "I want . . ."
>
> "I need . . ."
>
> "I prefer . . ."
>
> "I would like . . ."
>
> and, last, make sure that you are able to say "no" in several different ways. Practice these at home so that none are a struggle when you are in public situations. I have workshop'd this tutorial to both leaders and implementers.

Be gracious and be a clear communicator but get the information that you need. Think about what you most need to know in order to go forward with the prospective partner. That's a dating question, not a relationship query. You are not in a relationship yet but you do want to know deal breakers and Must Have kind of information. If they have certain opinions that are offensive to you and/or they don't care to hear a different point of view—your point of view—then you will probably judge them to be a poor date. Time to stop. Are you fairly solitary and need significant alone time? Maybe you are a sports fan and you, two, need to talk about how much game time is enough. Are you or the other person in the midst of personal chaos? Perhaps, you do not wish to relocate within the next ten years. Maybe that's okay. Maybe that's a deal breaker for the other person. Advance discussion questions: Do you both want children? How soon? Have you talked about parenting styles and what you believe in? Are you both good at personal finance?

Always be polite, of course. Don't grill or interrogate or even interview your prospective person. If negotiating simple matters like where to go on a next date shows you that you, two, are incompatible then remember to be gracious. Don't blame anyone for not being The One for You at This Time.

At this time, what is most important to you? What do you want?

Get clear about what you want. I cannot count for you the number of female clients that I've had who could not articulate a clear answer for themselves when I asked, "what do you want?" They want a man. They want a mate. They want to settle with someone and get on with living a life together. Males, too, just say that they want someone to love. They want someone who isn't too picky. They want to slide right into a relationship and things will just work out. Soon you are going to be in serious discussions with a prospective partner. This should not be the first time that you are thinking about what is most important to you.

What is the difference between wants and needs? Desires are your likes and preferences such as strawberry ice cream versus vanilla just because you like one more than the other. But desires are fluff blowing in the wind. I say this because preferences can be discussed and negotiated or even discarded. I like strawberry ice cream a lot but it is a treat, not a meal. I do not have to have it. You have plenty of room to negotiate where desires are concerned. She likes seafood and you do not or not very much, so, you prepare foods that you both like. Consider eating different entrees at the same meal sometimes. Try eating variations of the food that she likes most. You might surprise yourself. You can work with this.

A design consultant was once asked what a couple

should do if they had vastly different tastes in décor and wanted to live together. She said compromise on most rooms of the house so that you have a uniform look. Then, make sure that at least one room is strongly reflecting each person's style. Remember, desires can be worked with. He loves blue on the walls and synthetic floors and she loves oranges and natural wood floors. You want your beloved to have her desires met.

Needs are Must Haves. Must Haves mean you get to stay You or without them something of you is lost. Don't let that happen. Needs are different from desires, even strong desires. Understanding your own needs is an important conversation to have with yourself. Sit quietly for ten minutes and ask yourself, "What is most important to me?" Allow your Deepest Self to answer. Some possibilities are religious observance, remaining vegan, volunteer work, having children, not having children, sports and exercise, being outdoors in Nature. What's your list and why? The why's could have to do with health. I like vanilla ice cream. That's a desire. I stay away from strawberries and anything that has strawberries in it because my body doesn't do well with them. So, my partner needs to know that I won't be eating any strawberry ice cream. What if I am allergic to dog fur? Then, I guess my partner and I won't have a dog household <u>or</u> we will find a way around my suffering. These are things that can be discussed but they can't exactly be negotiated. If I need to continue my religious observances then I just do. The person that I am dating will need to determine for himself whether it is a deal breaker or not.

More determinants for Must Haves? Going to church/synagogue/mosque/temple regularly and that's because you identify as a religious person. It's says something about who you are. So, look out for identities or character traits that you want to protect. Not dating a smoker or someone who drinks a lot or someone who prefers bars when you do not may have to do with your high regard for living a healthy life. So, your Must Have list should include things to which you give super priority. Perhaps, you are avoiding people who hate bar culture when you thrive in it. I do not know what that says about you but I can generalize and say that your list should include high priority cultural environments. This could be cold weather camping, extreme sports, Frisbee competitions, language clubs and travel, singing and choral groups. Having children or not wanting to have children and wanting to be a very hands-on parent or not so much can be an identity item or cultural influence or it could represent some idea you have about contributing to the world. Think about it. Having time apart versus doing everything together is to be negotiated as part of how you will live together. Your need to handle your own money (or maybe you have no such need) and how you think about financial matters is to be negotiated. This last one may have to do with your ability to feel safe in the world. I've known several women who needed this.

Again, what do you want? Visualize your new relationship. See everyday scenes starring the two of you. See as much rich details as you can. Observe how good it feels to already be an Unequal Partnership-type partner. Now, let's go and find your beloved.

Chapter Four:
The Dating Pool and Dating Strategies

Where are you looking?

My book is not a dating guide in some general sense. You and I know that there are countless books that deal in depth with the subject of finding someone. I refer you to those other texts. Still, I want to say a few words about a general topic. I want you to consider the quality of where you choose to look. I hope that you are pursuing your desires and interests and by doing so you are surrounding yourself with people who like what you like.

For one thing, think about a broad search in a vertical direction. In tennis practice, we were encouraged to play against those who were our betters as a strategy for improvement and growth. Same thing with dating. Don't be shy about deliberately putting yourself in the big leagues to give yourself creative new possibilities for finding friends and dates. People network in the business world in precisely this way. Find out when your local college is having business mentorship meetings open to the public. Campuses are known for their art lectures and film festivals that are open to the public. Interest groups, not associated with the college, may just meet on the campus. TEDx conferences in my area meet on local campuses. Remember, if you pursue this tactic, that you are only trying to make new friends. Don't give off the energy of someone who is desperate or in any way in need. Behave yourself. Be the person that others would like to have as a real friend. Dating situations are most likely to follow.

I hope that you are doing your search broadly in the geographic sense too, of course, and not just in your local restaurants and bars. However, I cannot overlook the fact that a friend said that he found three of his girlfriends plus one good friend in his neighborhood grocery store. Fresh veggies, sliced cheese, and thee. I knew someone whose company was about to blow up on the international scene. He enrolled in Japanese language courses and committed himself to study with great success. He wanted to position himself professionally and personally to take advantage of the terrific possibilities coming his way. This man delightfully discovered that he had caught the eye of an executive in a different company who might never have noticed him if not for his extra efforts. He and his husband have enjoyed an Unequal Partnership for the past ten years.

Using vacations and business trips for multiple purposes is wise thinking. Scheduling vacations with dating strategies in mind is not unheard of. It can be one of the wisest things you ever did for yourself.

Where are you located?

Your own location may severely influence your availability. It may greatly distort what dating markets are available to you. I once knew a woman who lived on the side of a mountain in Washington State. She was in a remote area, to say the least. It took an hour and a half just to reach the valley below and another half hour to get to any sizable town. Grocery runs were not frequent. She described where she lived in an online profile. She made it clear that she expected her prospective mate to come and live with her. That was one tall order. But wasn't she right to ask in clear terms for what she really wanted?

Do you like where you live now? Do you have any aspirations to live elsewhere? Where? Are you willing to relocate for love?

Dating Strategies for Unequal Partnership Singles

Mine your familiar territory. Whom do you already know but you have not considered in a romantic way? Who is within your social scene and worth your time?

Don't discount your family neighborhood. Sometimes, there is a person who wasn't all grown up the last time that you gave them a thought. Maybe Little Jimmy has done a lot of work on himself since last you knew. Maybe he's Bartholomew Meadows, Ph.D., scholar, and bestselling author these days. Or, maybe he reinvented himself as Jake T., rapper and musicologist. Take a look around in your existing world.

If you take that look around in your world and there is no social set to peruse then forget about this stage in your dating plan and go back one step. Build up your friend network for your own sake. Volunteer in your community. Look around for where you are needed. Get your mind off YOU. See what you can give. When you've developed a real life and community for yourself, full of people who care about you and full of meaningful connections, then begin a new search for someone that you might want to make a life with. You will have a delightful world to share with your newfound love. That is not a small matter. Relationships, if they are meant to be lasting, need support from the outside. You need to be the kind of person who cares about contributing to your community. That's how you enrich yourself, enrich your most intimate relationship, and help your communities. You need community.

Your attitude should be that you want to have a rich world to offer your prospective mate. Never think of your intended loved one as a captured bird who'll be everything to you, who'll entertain you, sex you, and be all that you need. The captured-bird-in-a-cage scenario is not love, no matter how lovely the cage.

Go where your interests lead you. If you are happy within a faith institution then I can recommend that you think about whom you know and whom you'd like to get to know. Many people make their social life rooted in the church, synagogue, Buddhist temple, or mosque. I've known non-egalitarian relationship success stories that began within spiritual circles of one sort or another. I've known Wiccan couples who are happy with the leading partner/implementing partner model. Buddhists, Muslims, and Christians have stayed within their faith and practiced an Unequal Partnership. So give it a try if Unequal calls to you. That shy guy over there with a cookie crumb on his bottom lip might be the leader (or implementer) that you're looking for.

If you were a male who enjoys sewing or weaving, you would not have any trouble finding others with the same interest in my part of the country.

Or, I bet that the Saturday afternoon board game meetup has been a lot of fun for you. The group probably has given you new social friends and a few closer friends. You might have fertile ground for dating possibilities.

Go where "hierarchy" or "non-egalitarian relationship" might not be an unfamiliar subject. Polyamorous gatherings such as potlucks and meetups might be a start. Many of my clients are polyamorous. Some of my clients were simply looking for a partnership model that would inform their life answers. Unequal Partnership was a milestone direction to which to turn. No, you do not have to know for sure that you are not monogamous in order to attend such events. Just go and be your regular friendly self. It's also okay to be the monogamous life partner of someone who is polyamorous. Yes, it happens and people are happy. So, poly or monogamous, just be yourself and go and visit.

Take a look at BDSM events, conferences, and clubs. Yes, it's okay to go and take a look. You have my permission. No one will make you do anything that you don't want to do. Such places are super-concerned about safety. (You might be surprised by what you might like to think about doing.) I recommend that you start by creating email buddies who are knowledgeable and comfortable in the kink world. This is very easy to do online. Talk to people via the Internet. You'll very soon get a sense of who is safe to talk to. Be open about the fact that you are new. When you are ready, tell one of your online acquaintances that you would like to meet them at a "munch" (a simple, no pressure meet up at a restaurant. Nothing sexual or kinky happens. Strangers will be eating and talking. That's all. Some munches schedule guest speakers.) Here you can continue your journey of just learning by listening and watching. If a munch feels right to you then you can go again to your local munch or go to some other community's munch and make friends. When I was curious I deliberately chose a munch that was two hours from my home. I had a lovely time among friendly and welcoming people.

Remember, your job is to learn as much as you can. Please check the references at the end of this book. There is a wonderful literature to add to your education these days.

Go toward what your intuition is telling you and take your time. Make friends, which is easy. As you discover leading personalities that you can date if you know yourself to be on the implementing side or you find yourself drawn to implementing types because you are a leader-type then in the kink world you will not have to explain your desire for a non-egalitarian relationship. Proceed with happy dating experiences. Enjoy yourself. Oh, and about that kink thing? Well, if you stayed in the kink world long enough to date then it is going to occur to you that maybe there is something new in your life that's worth researching and seriously thinking about. Remember that everything is happily up for negotiation.

Last on this subject is the relationship conference. Not sexual. Not kinky. Not polyamorous. There are a small number of these, which are scattered throughout the United States. They have a series of presenters who delve into a myriad of relationship issues. There are always small group activities and panel discussions. Evenings are always filled with social gatherings for a really relaxing and fun time. It's easy to make friends. Large-scale religious institutions, sometimes, have these conferences. Otherwise, Internet searching is the way to go.

Shared activities. In my experience, first dates have more substance to them if there is a planned activity. Think of them as fun first and, secondly, as information gathering opportunities. Really. I want you to keep your questions in mind as you have a shared activity with someone whose company you can enjoy. I've taken dates to the botanic gardens, for long walks or hiking in the woods, for lunches, to museums, to galleries, and to festivals.

We're talking about lots of activity from which you have to choose. You can have as much or as little as you want. What do you like to do? Activities, things to do, are a good thing. A shared activity may be your first opportunity to experience each other's opinions, feelings, preferences, and reactions to a wide variety of situations.

Yes, many people live in social drought areas. This means having to travel. You might even have to schedule vacation time and jump on a plane. Use vacations and business trips to your personal advantage. That means staying alert to opportunities to make friends. I have. It can be one of the wisest things you ever did for yourself.

What to Look For:
How to <u>Listen</u> Your Way toward Your Mate

So, now, here you are feeling butterflies in the tummy because some boy or girl thinks you're hot. You've decided that your new person is a keeper. Great. How much do you know about this keeper? He's sweet, right? She's funny and intelligent and makes you coffee in the morning. Great. When it comes to decision-making what kind of behavior have you seen? How solid and reliable is this person? How partner-like are they? It's really a person's behavior that you want to use as the strongest determinant of whether you are going forward with Mr. or Ms. Sweet. Listen to your gut. Your intuition never lies, so, listen. There are plenty of good dating books to take it from here. But if you want to find good candidates for your heart's wish of a beautiful Unequal Partnership then learn to listen intuitively.

Listen inside yourself. Really. It's not magic. It's not science. It's your Inner Wisdom. Listen carefully. Without the ability to tune inward and without a good understanding of yourself, you are headed toward confusion even with a wonderful and well-chosen mate.[10]

"I choose with whom I will commit to spending my life, my heart, and my soul." I choose. The choosing is part science, in that there is plenty of research to refer to but the rest is discernment or showing yourself that you won't settle for anything less than excellent quality in a mate. You decide. Discernment is an internal listening skill plus having the strength to make a decision.

Listen to your prospective partner. What are they really saying to you? Are they willing to stretch with you and enter into a shared vulnerability? You have to take risks and be revealing of self as you move along with your prospective person. No risks, no gain. But at the same time, your ears and your intuition should be hearing that your prospective partner is willing to let down their barriers as well. Watch out. There are prospectives who want you to take all the risks. You would be putting yourself out there to be accommodating to them while they fearfully stay behind their walls. That's not partner material.

Listen. Your prospective partner deserves your full attention. It's an act of respect. It's the practice of good partnering skills that will get you closer and closer to the right Unequal life partner for you.

What to Look for:
<u>Feel</u> Your Way Toward Your Loved One

You can feel your way toward that right person for you. Feel, not think. Right now, imagine being your partner self. Be what you want to be today. Don't wait. Feel it. Taste it. Be your leader self. Be your implementing partner self. Be it now so that it is your partner self that the world sees. As you date, lead with what you are, either a leading partner type or an implementing partner type. Let that inner core, the True Self, shine so that your opposite can find you. It should feel great to step out on a date as The (Leading or Implementing) Partner Who Is Going to Find The Right Partner for Me. Each time that you go out on a date expand from your inner core as The Partner. Practice including your date in that expanded good feeling. This part is not a visualization but rather a feeling, an experience that is very real for you. You can have this full, satisfied feeling any time you want. I have had dates who were playing a much more guarded game than I was and must have wondered what was wrong with peaceful, joyous me. Actually, my loving nature was an invitation to them to come out and play with me. Some did and we had a fun evening and some just couldn't get away from me fast enough. Smile.

Pump yourself up by focusing on True Self. Daily, the world that you live in does not see the True Self nor does it want this from you. You have to protect yourself so you offer only a limited version of you. If you begin to get serious with the person you are dating then, among other things, you will have begun to be more and more revealing of self. Your partnering skills will have kicked in. You feel like it's okay to be vulnerable to a growing extent. You feel gradually safer with this person. Late in the game, you believe that you can share your secrets with this person. Can you? Partners share at a deep level. Can you?

You should be having countless experiences with the prospective mate who demonstrates loving acts and loving attitudes toward other people, not just you.

I dated a woman one time only because of her behavior during our first lunch together. She was dismissive, arrogant, brash, and domineering toward our waitress. That was it for me.

Choose someone who has demonstrated a generous heart and a kind, open spirit.

Feel your way toward your life partner:

1. Two persons are dating. She takes him home with her for Easter dinner. As soon as the couple walks through the door, they are confronted with a warm welcome from several cousins, including someone holding a newborn baby. The dating male immediately, genuinely reacts by asking, "May I hold her?" The dating female knew in her heart and by his actions that he was the guy she wanted to spend her life with. Twenty years later she, the leading partner, and he, the implementing partner, say that their marriage is still strong and interesting for them. That Unequal couple prioritizes feelings and being fully present for each other.

2. A prospective implementing partner noticed on his visits to see a prospective leading partner that she had a drawer full of single socks and mismatched socks. Another drawer had discolored undies and t-shirts. All of these were the result of poor laundry skills. His first smart move was to avoid criticizing her lack of domestic talent. Instead, he made sure that he was there on laundry day and asked to

take over laundry duties. She was grateful for his kindness. She was in romantic bliss whenever he monitored the wash while they watched movies and hung out on the sofa.

Given that relationships are a lot of work, choose someone who isn't afraid to work and who will work even harder when life isn't easy.

Pay attention to how you feel. Practice partnering, in a light sense, while you are dating. Ask yourself if you have been experiencing partnering with this person to whom you might commit. This is definitely a feel-your-way task. It makes sense to do the work of studying relationship dynamics (like reading this book), taking the time to develop good relationship skills, and assessing your real experiences with your prospective loved one. Your feelings are an internal natural guidance system. Use them for your own benefit.

Chapter Five:
You Can Find Your Leading Partner

The leading partner is the keeper (and for some couples he or she is the designer) of the meta level of the couple's way of living. The outer container, the product of the couple's agreements, is where we see

--A direction for the relationship,

--Largest goals like retirement decisions,

--Determining a social identity like one or both of you running for public office or being community volunteers,

--Forging a consistent, coordinated parenting style,

--And attention to maintaining the health of the relationship. So, let's look more closely at whom you'll need if you're looking for a leader personality.

You should hear in your prospective partner's conversations what framework that they are offering. What are the organizing principles that seem to drive their life? What's most important to them? What motivations and beliefs influence this person's life? I would be watching for, what in the ship analogy would be, a firm hand on the wheel. Do they seem to drift into talking about planning for the future fairly often? They enjoy thinking ahead, isn't that right? Do they seem to be consistent in their plan making? Are they planning without me or planning with me? Are they hearing my needs? I would want someone who solicits my opinions and I can clearly see that they value them.

This is someone who carries herself in an honorable way. You've witnessed their ethical behavior, sound decision-making, self-confidence, and kindness. If they say they are going to do something you can count on the task being done. "I feel good being with this dating friend in a deep way. This is a solid person. I feel safer."

Naturally, you want to hear their understanding of leading/implementing. How much slant of control or deference is the right prescription for the two of you is probably the big question that hangs in the romantic air. There is no single sentence or single conversation that fills in the blank here. You, two, will find your answers about the general shape of your relationship container over time and over many discussions. But as you enjoy being with your prospective partner, be attentive to the organizational elements pointed out in this book. It should seem to you that your prospective person is darn easy with organizational matters. At the same time, it should impress you that they are just being themselves.

I want to remind you of my True Self concept because I do not want anyone thinking that someone can study up and become a Leading Partner or an Implementing Partner. It just won't work. One of these personas is your true nature and inclination or it's not. I have had several prospectives who read my writings, loved what I had to say, and swore that the implementing partner position was the right place for them. Each was strongly inappropriate there. Each simply wanted what they wanted and was willing to horse trade for their needs. But that won't work. No one can role-play the part of leading or implementing. Either one of these is your truest expression of self or it's not. Absolutely every reader, though, can learn some very sound principles here for building a loving long-term relationship.

What if the person you are dating is just a really good person who has no experience taking the leading position in a committed relationship? Should you rule them out? If they really are good then they are honest. They will have read about the Unequal Partnership or some other model of non-egalitarian intimate relationship, felt a strong resonance with these ideas, and set out to find their implementing partner. Let's return to the ship/captain/first mate analogy for just a second. This person has never set sail with an Unequal Partner. This guy or woman with no actual life experience has no ship of his/her own. He or she is standing on the docks hoping to catch the eye of just the right prospective mate. Together they will set sail on rented boats until their experiences together lead them to commitment. That's when they build a ship together. Their agreements form the planks and machinery of their very own unique vessel. What a very fine analogy!

If you are okay with giving this no-experience person a try based on their honesty, first, and sweet face, second, then great. Move forward. That is, move forward if and only if 1) they propose a plan for learning together and 2) you find their plan acceptable. Any plan should include lots of reading and discussion. Please see my reference page.

I'm Hoping that You are <u>My</u> Leading Partner

You want to see self-assurance, self-respect, and evidence that self-development is important. Trust your first impression. If the person that you are considering walks into the restaurant and you realize that you barely noticed them then this person probably is not your best prospect. I know some very happy couples whose leading partner carries little public presence in my eyes. But you know what? The person has to be strongly present in <u>your</u> eyes, not mine. Your Innermost Self should stir when he/she is near. That may very well happen just a little bit later in your dating experience.

As you already know, not all dominant personalities are leading partner material by the concepts and principles of the Unequal Partnership model. I have to add that not all Unequal leading partners are right for you either. All of my discussions here have the purpose of helping you to focus, to zoom in on <u>your</u> right leading partner. That's all that matters.

Be sure to consult your Deal Breakers list one more

time, just in case, as a reminder to yourself. These are the traits or conditions that would absolutely turn you away. As I've written earlier, it's a good idea to start with these in mind on your dating journey. I had a prospective that showed up at our restaurant meet up in torn pants and a dirty shirt. In his conversation, he told me that he was a recreational drug user. He did not realize that he'd crossed into deal breaker territory on many counts for me.

Also, just as important, are your Must-Haves-In-the-Other-Person. While these are very closely linked to your deal breakers, they constitute a different list. This is an opportunity to dig deep inside yourself and realize what your Innermost Self is calling for. I happen to love this conversation with self/Self. There are at least two ways to look at Must-Haves-in-the- Other-Person:

1. Traits that the other person has outside of the relationship model such as wearing a full beard, or having a doctorate, or knowing auto mechanics. I knew a woman who insisted that her person had to come into the relationship debt-free. That was a good one. Or, what about "I must have someone who shares my religion and wants a non-egalitarian relationship."

2. A single special trait that you want the other

person to have that you <u>do</u> associate with the relationship model. Whatever answers come to the surface do not have to be rational or rational sounding. They just are. Here are some examples:

    ---Perhaps, you feel a deep thrill inside when you relate to a big-bodied, physically strong person with a dominant personality,

    ---Perhaps, what your Innermost Self is hungry for is a big-brain intellectual,

    ---Maybe, at the top of your list is a very spiritually-oriented person,

    ---Maybe, an energetic, fun, goofy personality would do nicely, or

    ---A sports lover is what gets your gut excited.

Mostly, we think of the Implementing Partner as having a single, deeply-held notion of who the leading partner is. However, the leading partner might be just as likely to mentally hold a one-to-one association of a certain trait with what it means to be an Implementer. I had a male client who could only visualize implementing partners as female and in high heels.

Chapter Six:
You Can Find Your Implementing Partner

You do not want just any available dating partner. You are playing the dating game as a precise strategy for finding your right implementing partner. The implementing partner takes your mutually held goals and runs with them. You want a good follow-through kind of person. Some couples think of the implementer's focus on implementation as taking the lead <u>inside</u> the relationship container and that's a fine way to judge what they do. You want your partner to be fully present and active in decision-making as opposed to leaving it all to you. Your implementing partner must be able to function fully for the good of the family without you being present every minute.

You want to see self-assurance, self-respect, and evidence that self-development is important. All of these traits equal healthy self-efficacy as opposed to dependency or codependency. Learn to recognize the difference.

Listen carefully to how your date describes their life. Do they have close friends and other successful, long-term relationships? These should be real friends. These should not just be friendly co-workers or people they see only at the bowling alley or at pick-up basketball once a week.

Where does this prospective person live? And what are conditions in his home like? I knew someone who had to say goodbye to a prospective partner because his supposedly amazing home was filthy and hadn't been cleaned in years. He wanted her to see it as their home, nonetheless.

Do they badmouth past partners or do they go out of their way to not be blaming and negative? Sometimes bad mouthing runs along gender lines: "most men are beastly and stupid," "females are worse off without a man in their lives," "people are backward and closed minded not to realize that human sexuality goes beyond binary gender." I hope that you are not tempted to join in the negativity: "Yeah. My wife treated me like that. She never got out of bed to do anything."

How well does the prospective partner speak up about

their needs? How able are you to assist and reassure them? Do so in a kind and gracious manner that instills trust.

Of course, you want to see your prospective partner responding easily to your lead once you've gotten to know each other fairly well. Expect an increasingly easy flow between you. When this happens, your heart swells further. Your abilities as leading partner are more evident to you and to your prospective partner.

What is their physical condition? Are there any medical issues, physical or mental? Either way, what matters is that the person is clear about what they are dealing with. They should want you to be able to make informed choices. Do they exercise and does that matter to you?

Where is the evidence that they genuinely care about others? The evidence lies with how they behave with other people, not you. I've had dates that could not tolerate children. I consider that a bad sign. Maybe, you do not. I've had one or two dates who thought that mentoring others or volunteering in one's community was for chumps. They were the chumps that I dismissed from my dating life.

I'm Hoping that You are <u>My</u> Implementing Partner

We were making plans to go to a concert. I, the leading partner, had put together the rough details like having checked with him that he was available that night and that he wanted this to happen as much as I did. We were talking on the phone another time and as we continued to share our opinions and thoughts about that particular concert performer, my guy was typing away on his laptop and got us our tickets. He initiated further conversation about what else we were going to need for an outdoor concert like a cooler for snacks and buying a sun tent. A sun tent. Smile. I would not have thought of that. That's my guy.

Know what your Deal Breakers are and be honest enough to discuss these openly and early.

Write down your own Must-Haves-in-the-Other-Person. Look at your list, which should be short if it is to be realistic. Now, keep these in mind but hold them loosely, not with a closed-minded determination aimed at finding exactly what you wrote on your list.

What do you already know about personality types that you have dated and enjoyed or strongly disliked? Some leader types think of bratty behavior as cute and self-actuated. What is your reaction? Some like quiet, peaceful personalities. How has your taste evolved based on your past dating history? Remember that you are not looking for merely someone that you think that you might get along with. Rather, you want a well-formed adult who aligns with your personality and with whom you have the best chance at creating a wonderful Unequal Partnership.

What kind of energy and awareness does the prospective person show in various situations? :

Marcus X, age 50, had formed a very low energy, take-few-risks life for himself. He saw no reason to change or modify anything. And yet he fully expected companionship that suited his tastes. There was no concern for the other person's needs. When asked he said that the way that he did things "should be good enough."

Notice when you feel most leader-like in your personal life. Can you associate this feeling with any people traits? For instance, at the movies, a gentle hero(ine) comes on the screen and your leaderly energy rises with intensity but then softens, leaving you a vulnerable puddle. Strong and soft. Don't worry. No one in the movie theater took notice. Or, the hero part of a television show comes on and you see yourself as that hero saving the day for some curly haired, dimple-cheeked just-right partner for you. Was it the dark curly hair or the dimples that did it for you?

If you are a leader-type do you find yourself drawn to in charge/get it done types? Well, good. You are not looking for someone who has no mind of his or her own. You want a strong and able, mature adult to complement your own strengths. As you date, notice how well that prospective partner relates to you. You want to see and feel them respond to your leader-type qualities. You should feel fantastic. It should feel as though your entire inner self is welling up. That's your leaderly energy rising to the surface again and again. Thinking about when you are at your most leaderly is an awareness that will help to steer you toward your right life partner. While you're riding high, I am sure that you also took notice of whether the prospective implementing partner is high and happy, too.

You, the prospective leading partner, must talk explicitly about control in the relationship. You should really like and enjoy the prospective implementing partner's reactions to what you have to say. It should be part of your shared dating pleasure to watch their reactions to how you handle yourself in one situation after another.

I guess that I better tell you that you are not required to know all the answers all the time. Instead, try staying relaxed, just be yourself, and trust yourself to make good decisions as you go along. Your prospective implementing partner will show great appreciation for your honest expression of who you are.

Chapter Seven:
A Few Dating Snafus and Combinations

Power Deference Questions

If you thought to ask your potential Significant Other what his favorite color is or if she is into sports, did you also think to ask a Power Deference Question? These are for everyone:

In previous relationships who made most of the decisions and how were they made?

Did you and your ex- have an explicit agreement about sharing responsibilities or did things just kinda happen?

If you and your ex- lived together who was the Designated Handler of Personal Finances? Or, did you keep your finances separate?

Are you someone who likes to be in charge?

What happens when you don't get your way?

Do you prefer to make joint decisions?

Do you think of yourself as a collaborator?

Where were you in the birth order?
Did you get along with your siblings?
How close are you to family now?

Do not interrogate your date. Just hold these questions in mind. These questions are intended to be a helpful start in thinking about how power and control affect your date's behavior and your own. Let them inform your thinking as you interact with one date after another.

Dating Combinations

As you and Ms. Sweet proceed to have experiences together you will notice, in your behavior and hers, one of the following combinations relative to power and control. I'm going to use a popular shorthand (that is already in the literature) of **D** for leading partner and **S** for implementing partner:

D + S: this is great. Leading partners are looking for implementing partners and vice versa. They can offer each other love and stability.

D + ?, S + ?: Unequal partner roles are based on

natural proclivities; your dating friends are what they are. The dating pool is full of pleasant dating possibilities for each of you but not every leading or implementing prospective is going to be the right one that you need. My "?" is for the terrific person who isn't the right partner for you. I know. Sad because you spent your time dating them and you really enjoyed their company but he/she is not right for you.

S + S: these are two people who are not in their comfort zone when it comes to making big decisions. Each procrastinates and they procrastinate as a couple together: "Whatever you want, Sweetheart." "Oh, no, my darling. I want you to have what _you_ want." "I feel the same way, Precious. Whatever _you_ want." Egalitarian is the way to go here plus regularly paying for outside decision helpers like an accountant, bankers, a financial manager, a lawyer, and a relationship counselor. I had clients, S + S, who have been happily married for more than thirty years so it is possible.

D + D: it is possible that two leading-types can be attracted to each other. That's a hard one. The solution is always being conciliatory and egalitarian. Yes, egalitarian. I know a handful of couples that fit this. These couples are married and happy.

The Watch Out!! Bin

'D + S' or 'S + D' and that sounds good, but what if she or he just isn't the right person for you? You're the D and she is the cutest S but not the one for you. You're the S and he/she is the most amazing D but not the one for you. New Relationship Fever can be blinding. People commit to the wrong person for all kinds of well-intentioned reasons.

S + S. You fall in love and commit to each other. It happens. You should find outside help for the big decisions as I discussed above. For example, they should have an accountant or money manager to help with their financial decisions. A counselor or a therapist can help with family decisions.

D + D. You fall in love and commit to each other. It happens. The solution is some form of egalitarian arrangement. Perhaps, each of you takes the lead in particular parts of your life together.

A Few Dating Snafus for Everyone

(These really happened.)

1. Mind Reading. It's <u>not</u> a Relationship Thing.

An implementing partner told her leading partner that he wasn't leaderly enough for her. He took a deep breath and checked himself for kindness, gentleness, and patience. He asked her what she wanted. She said that she couldn't find the words for it but he should just know (and, thus, prove to them both that he is her natural and proper leader).

2. I'm leading, I think.

"You should be happy since I'm doing the best I can." This one illustrates poor communication between the partners. No one is asking the leading partner to be robotically right all the time. Keeping a positive attitude and keeping up good communication with your partner are what's most important. "You should be happy since I'm doing the best I can" doesn't sound too good. Surely, the leading partner isn't expecting the implementing partner to accept whatever he/she dictates? That would not be very partner-like, would it?

I'm sorry but if you are an implementing-type, please, don't expect every leading type out there to be a great match for you. And the same goes for the leading types looking for an implementer. Some prospectives will feel so almost-just-right. Remember to <u>feel</u> your way toward your just-right partner. <u>Listen</u> your way in. When you arrive at your intended destination, your Innermost Self will say, "Aaah."

3. Wow. Follow Through was Hot and Cold.

We had our Saturday all planned. First of all, he, the prospective implementing partner, and I had agreed to meet at the beer garden at a specific time. We'd planned to end our night by driving to his house for our first stay over visit. He was very late without calling or without explanation. His attitude was "what's the big deal?" Second, the next morning there was nothing for me to eat. Breakfast for him but nothing for me. He did offer me coffee when he made some for himself. "If I'd thought about it, I would have remembered that you need gluten-free. I know a store where they sell gluten-free bread."

4. The Big Bad Match.

A prospective implementing partner said, "She sure is

picky or something. Why can't we just put the food on the table and just sit down and eat? Why do we have to have napkins or flowers or even conversation?" Just a bad match.

5. Another Bad Match.

I met a prospective implementing partner at a restaurant. He was polite but distant at first and for quite some time. He began to tell me about himself as one long monologue: that he was former military, former Special Forces, trained interrogator, trained sniper. By this time, I knew that the right thing to do was to get out of there as fast as I could stand up and run out of the restaurant. I didn't. I hung in. Turns out that he was a big-hearted guy who dearly loved his volunteer work with troubled teens. He and I were just a poor match. The "I could kill you ten different ways" speech was just nerves. Bad match.

Chapter Eight:
Dating Went Well. Now, We Negotiate for Real.

What is the difference between negotiation in the business world and negotiation in the very personal partnership world?

The primary difference is that business negotiations pit the two persons against each other in order to get individual needs met and intimate partnership negotiations do not. In business, it's assumed that one person achieving what they want can only be done through the other person's loss or sacrifice. The intimate partnership has the partners necessarily working closely together as a unit in order to discover their needs as a whole and to design solutions for meeting those needs. The aim of intimate partnership negotiations has to be the discovery of all needs with a positive conclusion for all. The conclusion is an honest attempt to meet all needs and leave both parties better off <u>and</u> closer together.

Business negotiations are by design adversarial. In business negotiations, each person is in competition against the other to get their needs (demands?) met. There is an expectation of one person getting what they need at the expense of the other person. Neither is expected to have any concern for the other person's needs. There is an expected push-and-pull in the discussions in order to get as much of the individual's list met as possible. Both of two opposing sides are thinking in just this way.

In business negotiations, concessions are made but only in self-interest. Compromises are forged, also in self-interest, but getting as much as you can for yourself is the target. "Don't leave money on the table" is an often-heard phrase. There might be an adherence to social rules of business civility but if more of an emotional connection than that happens, it is unexpected and not required. Emotional outburst, tearfulness, or a show of affection and concern are usually thought of as undesirable. Emotional display only muddies the waters in a business environment.

The entire culture and traditional setup of business negotiations are aimed at ownership and/or the control of property. Objects and land and use rights are privileged over the emotional needs and quality of life of people. There is no such thing as attention given to emotional closeness between the two negotiating parties.

A trained mediator, an HR person, a court magistrate or a lawyer acting as mediator might conduct the business negotiation sessions. Or, if mediation is held within a company, the mediator is usually an HR consultant or someone who out ranks the two parties in dispute with each other.

Prospective life partners negotiate on their own. If they are having trouble or have questions they might turn to a close friend to help them or a trusted community elder such as a spiritual leader.

Intimate partnership negotiation has the purpose of discovery. It is never adversarial. The two persons, in initial formal negotiations, are saying, "Let's discover the truth about whether we can be together." If negotiations prove that the deal breakers are insurmountable or the prospective partners don't wish to try to overcome them then the work of negotiating has done its job. In this case, the two walk away graciously and wish each other well. Or, the conclusion may be that they might decide to stay in each other's lives but have no intentions of trying to move toward a life partnership. These are possibilities where one is a leader type and the other is an implementing type but negotiating has shown them that they are not the right match for each other. Having reached the partnership negotiation stage of dating is not in itself a guarantee that two dating friends should go forward into a committed relationship. Intimate partnership negotiations:

        1. Reveal each person's needs and wants and

        2. Set up discussions about the terms by which the two agree to go forward.

The leading partner has probably discussed her thoughts about Unequal Partnership early on. The prospective partners probably have most of the basics and the deal breakers already dispensed with in the earliest conversations. A first understanding of the framework or structure of Unequal Partnership that the leader is offering has already been discussed and agreed upon. For a couple that has been dating for quite some time and feels pretty solid together, it seems reasonable to move on to formal partnership negotiations:

---Revealing needs at a much deeper level and

---Agreeing on living conditions for going forward.

Negotiations for a relationship have to be thorough. Negotiations often conclude with a written contract.

Process: how to negotiate

Partnership negotiation happens only after a long series of dating conversations have been fruitful. You, two, have been dating for quite some time and have had many wonderful partial negotiations. Perhaps, during your dating phase, you negotiated over how to handle a particular, very specific situation like travel plans or meeting the relatives for the first time. Now, both parties believe that they might be a good bet as life partners. They do formal negotiations and get to a good level of detail about what being together will mean for their lives. At this stage, there really shouldn't be any surprises. You have already heard all of the deal breakers. You each liked what you have been experiencing with the other person. You've grown very close plus you've had many experiences that give you both a reason to believe that you are handling well the business of an intimate relationship. You've decided to move forward.

The steps leading to the door of partnership negotiation might look something like: email correspond-dence, telephone conversations, and then lots of in-person experiences, which become increasingly partner-like. Lots of communication is the key.

Partnership negotiation requires that the person in lead position must design a negotiation process. For example, the two might meet over lunch or dinner several times before beginning to write their contract. The leader declares the terms of the negotiation process and clearly communicates those terms for review by the other partner. The prospective implementing partner has every right to ask for modifications and to ask for conditions that will increase their comfort. The two of you would settle on conditions that make both of you as comfortable and at ease as possible.

Partnership negotiations probably include some written correspondence or readings or other aids to clarify what is meant. Prospective partners of mine have happily read my essays plus relationship books that I've recommended. It all helped toward gaining a shared perspective. I've used a shared document in Google Docs in the past. It was so easy to make corrections, to see changes, and to share notes. I love the written word for clarifying my own thinking as well as being clear about the other person's thinking.

The leading partner has the responsibility of creating a feel good environment for their discussions. Both persons have the right to conditions that are kind, patient, gentle, and understanding. Both should expect respect at all times.

One prospective leading partner invited his prospective implementing partner to lunch one day. He showed up at her place of work with a picnic basket. He had made sandwiches and salad for them. He'd baked blueberry muffins and made lemonade. He had real plates and cloth napkins. He was ready to negotiate. She had written a list of what was most important to her plus a poem that showed her feelings. She was ready to negotiate. She, later, said that she loved the effort that he had made on their behalf.

The leader should be ready to encourage the implementing partner to respectfully speak their mind throughout negotiations. Both partners should feel that it's easy to be revealing. The emotional environment should be open and unrestricted.

The leading partner must come to negotiations prepared to explain what structure they are setting for the nature of the relationship. Just as a house has walls and a roof and a foundation, the leading partner takes responsibility for leading them into a pretty well-defined relationship structure. This should have been explained in some part in earlier conversations. Being articulate about relationship structure is an important job that falls mostly on the shoulders of the prospective leading partner. This is not to say that the leading partner should have all the answers or have created a detailed plan. But it is to say that there is a show of leadership to be made in broad strokes at this early stage. Whatever the leading partner has to say about how they think the relationship might proceed should be received like any proposal for action. The prospective implementing partner is expected to respond directly to what they are hearing and with their own ideas, desires, and needs. Here, partnering looks like a wonderful free sharing of how the two of you feel about how to live your life together.

Once inside the door of partnership negotiation, the two of you will hold an intention of acting as a team focused on finding ways to meet all needs. Each prospective partner feels like a guardian of the other person's needs. As such they do not experience an inner conflict over whether their own individual needs will get met. This may seem like an unusual level of vulnerability. It is. It's what partners do.

Often, we find that the implementing partner isn't as forthcoming as they could be about their needs because they think that speaking up is not being very supportive. Or, that out of respect they should stay pretty humble. They think that they should just listen. They often are not aware or are unclear about what their rights are with any leading partner. Implementing partners are expected to participate fully in the negotiation process in order to give their prospective leading partner the best possible information about relationship sustainability. Furthermore, the implementing partner should participate fully in order to give herself/himself the best possible chance at creating terrific conditions for the beginning of a relationship.

In partnership negotiations both persons are taking great risks. They allow themselves to be vulnerable with another person. That's as it should be. Partnership negotiations require both persons to throw on the table all that they can pull out about their needs, desires, feelings, and hopes. It is the combined set that allows the two—not just the leading partner—to see if they are an excellent match. Of course, each prospective partner wants to feel assurance about committing. Negotiation is good for clarity.

Because the leading partner is responsible for setting the overall structure for negotiations and for how they will go forward in a relationship, it may appear to the reader that the leading partner is dictating terms to the implementing partner. There may be an assumption that the implementing partner has little control or comparatively less control. But, in fact, the implementing partner has most of the control. Only they dictate how much control that they are willing to give to their leading partner. Also, they must act as a negotiating partner and give their information and react fully to the terms that the leader is offering. Partnership negotiations are always about deriving truth. The two persons want the truth of whether they can move forward together. Manipulation or power grabs or dictating terms has no place in what it means to partner.

"Partnering" does not mean equal responsibilities for all things. It does mean shared responsibilities. Remember, the overall goal is personal happiness, not drudgery. Can they act together each with their very different set of responsibilities to form something amazing in the world?

Here, I have only discussed the first formal negotiation. But I will repeat that the partners always, always have an expectation of negotiating again and again. Some Unequal Partnership couples write a contract with an end date (say, of one year), which forces them to have new discussions and to renew their commitment to each other in an active way. Either person at any time can call for a new negotiation period. Negotiating attempts to take care of all the needs for the couple. Negotiation is not for one person's gain instead of the other's. Unequal partners do not allow one person to sacrifice his or her needs. The goal is always to create conditions for the personal happiness of all partners.

Sometimes, those early discussions weren't looking good but you two began negotiations anyway. It's more than okay for the partners to say, "Thank you. I enjoyed our time together. I don't feel that we can push past our political differences/religious differences/philosophical and moral differences." If the implementing partner feels strongly about receiving communion/meditating daily/saying prayers at bedtime or at the table and the leading partner has no interest in this then the partners probably need to look elsewhere. Politics or money issues can tear an otherwise compatible couple apart so the question will be do you say goodbye or do you work hard and creatively to make both of you happy with the differences intact. As another example, if the leader insists on being studious and discussing things as the norm in a personal relationship but the implementing partner hates to read and thinks a certain level of discussion is boring then they might want a different kind of leading partner whose emphasis is elsewhere. Regularly attending public events might be a deal breaker or it might be negotiable. Living together might be a deal breaker for either person. These issues and more are usually revealed long before the two reach formal negotiations and creating a contract but maybe not. Partnership negotiations are always a win-win even when the two must face the truth that there isn't enough connection and compatibility to sustain a relationship.

Partners have the right to expect absolute honesty:

I once had a partner who had a mental illness but he had not disclosed this to me. For one year, I was exposed to the symptoms of that illness with no way of understanding what was going on. The other person refused medical help and refused to admit that anything peculiar was happening. I know many people who are in long-term relationships with someone who has a serious physical or mental illness. In my case what was at issue was not the illness but rather that someone was being less than honest. (Yes, he knew that he was ill.)

What is the leading partner looking for during negotiations?

o Ease in working together.

o Compatibility.

o They are looking for a person whose interests and motivations complement theirs but also support their leadership in multiple ways.

- The leader wants to see that they can navigate the boat in conjunction with this person toward the fulfillment of their mutually shared goals.
- The leader wants to believe that they can aid, guide, or, otherwise, give support to their prospective partner's personal growth.
- They want to see that they can be vulnerable with this person.

The implementing partner is very concerned and protective of the leader's wants and needs. They bring a fresh honesty and they bring their most revealing self. They step up by keeping track of agreements. They step up by helping to see where some creative thinking sometimes will bring shared happiness. It's all in their nature, right?

What is an implementing partner looking for during negotiations?

- Assurance that they are safe and protected,
- Assurance that it's okay to be themselves and that they can be revealing and vulnerable,
- Assurance that the two of you can share in a deep way,
- They want to see that their input is just as important as the leading partner's,

• They want to feel that their implementing perspective is needed, even crucial.

The leading partner stays focused on the implementing partner's needs. Before, during, and after negotiations the leading partner sees to the comfort of the implementing partner. The leader steps up by helping to see where some creative thinking sometimes will bring shared happiness. It's all in their nature, right?

Together, what are the partners making agreements about? Here are some possibilities:

1. What is our essential reason for being together? Companionship, for instance. Pursuit of personal happiness for you both. A business reason like sharing resources or securing citizenship.

2. Commitment to a non-egalitarian relationship model.

3. Decision-making model: dictatorial or somewhat inclusive or inclusive.

4. Whether they will live together. Some very successful couples do not live in the same house. Or, some are those who delay moving in together in order to work on other aspects of the relationship first.

5. Where to live together. My house or yours or buy a house

together? Choose an entirely new location? Move to Denmark or Venezuela?

6. Who will work and bring in an income? Who will continue their career? Who has an opportunity to pursue creative choices and can we make that healthy for both of us?

7. How will we have checks and balances in our relationship? How will we check on ourselves and the health of the relationship as we go along?

8. Are there outside responsibilities that cannot be helped like caring for an elderly parent and how will we accommodate this in our life together?

9. Do we want children right away? Who will be the designated hands-on caretaker or guardian if one or both of us has to travel for work? How will we support each of us as parents? How can we seek support in our community for us as parents?

10. What are our core values? How do we pledge to live together? Here are possibilities:

> **Honesty** – Being honest at all times will maximize our understanding of one another. We want to avoid passive-aggressive behaviors, as these combine two

unattractive traits: dishonesty and an unwillingness to communicate directly.

Dedication – By nature, this is destined to be an intense relationship. It takes dedication and commitment to keep it a satisfying experience for both parties.

Respect – Mutual respect is the cornerstone of any relationship. Each of us will respect limits and matters of safety for the other. Each of us will respect the expectations of the other, . . . [11]

11. If we have a difference of opinion or an actual dispute, how will we deal with it and reset peace? How shall each of us register dissatisfaction and suggest a change?

12. Do we expect to do everything together or have friends to do things with separately sometimes?

13. Do we expect to change over time? Do we expect to have to deal with change in each other over time?

14. What exactly are our individual responsibilities? What do you expect of me?

15. Do we expect each of us to be punctual?

16. Do we care about how we look in public? Or, is appearance not important?

17. Do we have anything to say to each other about how we conduct ourselves with other people?

18. Are we monogamous or polyamorous? Do we wish to consider an open relationship? What information do we need in order to make the best decision for us?

19. Do we want to say anything to each other about general hygiene, staying healthy, and seeing a doctor?

20. What are our expectations about sexual activity with each other?

21. What are our expectations about communication with each other?

22. Contract? How often shall we review our contract? Renew or not and how?

These are just suggestions. You will choose what works for you. I think that you should write down all of your main agreements. If there is a written contract or something less formal, either way, then the partners can look at that document with pride---this is us.

Partnership negotiations tend to be a warm, cozy intimate affair. Sometimes, neither partner feels that there is much to discuss once the deal breaker conversations are over. But, of course, there are a lot of issues going forward. Sure. Negotiations can be a slam-bang business and the new couple can get on with the fun. Or, the process can be slower. Either way, there is no slogging through here. I once conducted negotiations in my two-person bathtub. Several long walks in a forest on a summer's day would probably take care of everything. The point is to set a kind and loving tone with each other. Again, I will say that as you go forth into your wonderful future as a healthy, happy Unequal Partnership, you can and will negotiate again and again as needed. It will be your pleasure to do so.

Chapter Nine:
Deeper Negotiations
(Because This Beautiful Thing is Working)

Deeper. Let's take our thinking deeper, deeper still:

Who do we think we are together and what do we want? What are our hearts' desires?

What are our fundamental needs? Other needs?

What are our goals just for today because Life is pressing on us and dictating need?

Otherwise, what are our goals as a couple?

What are some of the details for operating as a healthy, coherent unit in the world?

What's our process for answering any of these questions?

How do we approach decision-making with deliberateness and kindness?

If we want X, a short-term or a long-term goal/desire/need, then how do we get there from here? Let's practice planning right now.

The Relationship Contract

Here is what I have to say about creating a contract. It's your agreements set down in writing. It's one of your best tools on the way to building a sustainable relationship. We have good social science research on this. Americans don't seem to want to believe that it's true. Or, rather, American couples have a mindset that's stuck on thinking that "contract" is a business tool and "business" is not romantic, and that, in fact, it's anti-romance. You have now read my book. Thank you. I hope that my arguments here have helped you to have a broad mental framework as you approach your own Unequal Partnership. I hope that you are headed toward your own Unequal Partnership or, at a minimum, you have gained some good relationship tools and insights. Contracts can help you whether you are or not. Relationship contracts are a personal matter; they are not legally binding.

The process of writing down your most important agreements is a strong tool for any new couple. Now that I've told you that it is a good thing to do, I'm going to surprise you by saying that it is okay to set the contract in the drawer and only look at it a year from now. You will appreciate seeing how far you've come during your first year. You will appreciate your deep sincere effort to establish a solid partnership---an Unequal Partnership.

Allow me to briefly describe a traditional way to use a contract:

---write down your major agreements. This constitutes the framework or container within which you are saying that you are determined to live. Don't be afraid to work on evolving drafts until you have it just right for you. Don't overdo the process, though. Creating a contract should not become a pain in everybody's side. Enjoy seeing yourselves progressing along.

---create an exit clause at the end of your final draft. An exit clause describes how each of you would like to be treated if the relationship must end. Some individuals would like to receive a long love letter from their partner telling them about their feelings. Some people say that they just want a long series of reasonable conversations if the relationship is to end. Some people want a final conversation with a relationship counselor as a witness. (In one incidence, bringing a relationship to a close included gentle conversations and then a final one in the office of a counselor.) The idea of imagining a back door for an intimate relationship is pretty weird. It is. But love cannot be held too tightly. The idea that each of us will be safer and more secure against heartbreak if we hold the beloved in a tight grip is a poor one. The too-tightly-held idea just doesn't work in any relationship. Instead, building the tools and practices of partnership and living them constantly is the stuff of shared reality. In this way, we sidestep building insecurity into a relationship. Consider writing a relationship contract.

Almost fifty percent of American marriages end in divorce.[12] Many of them ended in an emotionally violent way. Wouldn't it be impressively loving that if necessary you left each other in a better position, as much as possible, to go on with your lives? Please write an exit clause. Just a few lines will do. If the time ever comes and you have to refer to it then your shared purpose is to treat each other lovingly, just like you did at the start of the relationship.

Here is a very basic agenda:

---Write down your most important agreements.

---Create an end for the contract. Typically, this would be a year after its start. Your intention here is to celebrate your anniversary. Celebrate your love. Celebrate your freedom to choose what you want and what will make you happy. Celebrate your ability to choose each other again. Show gratitude for your wonderful love no matter what you choose to do. I know an implementing partner who jokes about how great it is to be free for 48 hours each year: "I can go wild and do anything I want!" That couple has been solid for fourteen years and counting with fourteen contracts behind them.

---Write a new contract for the next new period. Hurray for love.

I believe in relationship contracts. Please check the book's end for more information about how to create a relationship contract.[13]

Conclusion: Loving within Structured Walls

If this is your right person, if this is The Partner for You, then you will have noticed an easy partnership forming over time. You'll have discovered how sexy your constructive discussions can be. Instead of work and drudgery it feels great to form agreements. The structure you're creating with your partner will deliver on all the happiness you can imagine in a sustainable loving Unequal Partnership.

I'll shout it again: the business of partnership is the firmament of love and romance. Build relationship structure to hold all those feelings – – – you know, the hot and delicious ones that you have now plus the up and down feelings that are predictably going to fluctuate throughout your years together. Build a fabulous container from your well-made agreements. By doing so you'll always have walls, foundation, and a roof to protect you and family as the good and not so good stuff of life happens in your direction. Unequal Partners are in a continuous daily practice of thinking and working as a unit.   When life happens they are smooth as a team taking care of business. You will never ever be starting from zero with your decision-making in <u>any</u> situation. You and your beloved will have the structure that you built to fall back on. You'll be able to find your answers . . . together.

Remember that I spoke of dating as your personal system for discovery? Therefore, it is not an end in itself but rather a proving ground for whether you should launch the next gigantic stage in your life. You do not hunger for guarantees. You know now to ride your intuition and your discernment toward the truth. You and your new partner think that you can and should give it a shot and so that's your shared truth. Your aim is partnership. That's truth. Dating in its late stages has transformed itself into partnering. You, two, have been practicing partnering and things are going very well. You no longer need the training wheels of dating. Instead, transformation looks like good and continuous communication in place with little effort; it looks like frequent discussion of the things that matter held in great trust; it looks like your agreements forming a healthy container to hold you from here and going forward. You each know to hold your responsibilities in the relationship as sacred. No one and nothing comes before your life partner. **Lean in** and hold each other dearly.

I promise to write about the Unequal Partnership in even more detail in the second and third books in the series.

I am still entertained by romantic comedies, by the way. You would think that I would not be able to stand them but some of the movies are still funny to me. It is my hope that my relationship model gave you more options to consider than the Boyfriend/girlfriend scenario as represented in romantic comedies. I am imagining that my Unequal Partnership model offered you something substantial, a lot to chew, and a different portrayal of how things can work between two loving and mature adults.

The Unequal Partnership model offers a different set of standards to judge what is possible in your relationships relative to your own personal happiness. It's a constructive set of standards that I hope more and more people use or are informed by whether they are Unequal Partners or not. My prayers and my work are aimed at challenging your expectations about intimate relationships. Plan. Make plans. It's my wish that my books help you and others re-design your plans so that you are more likely to get that life of peace and happiness that you are really wanting. Thank you and best wishes to you.

Aisha-Sky Gates, http://gatescounseling.com

About the Author

Aisha-Sky Gates, author and relationship coach, created the Unequal Partnership model based on experiences with her many contented clients. She writes on many topics, including successful loving relationships and a variety of alternative lifestyle choices.

http://gatescounseling.com

Addendum 1:
A Submissive Looking for a Caring Dominant

This is a real person's statement. Thank you to L.

When I am single, I tread murky waters and try to keep my head above temptations that will lead me to feeling like a used doormat. I set an intention to take good care of myself. I also need to balance self-care and introversion with getting out and socializing with friends and other single people. When I get out, I like warm greetings, especially hugs.

Socializing generally results in finding someone who I can serve, someone who I can please. I have to fight the temptation to immerse myself in submitting to meeting the needs of another, at least until I have determined that this lucky person is reciprocally interested in meeting my needs. So I need boundaries to protect myself, at least until I find an appropriate match.

What is the right match for me?

I am seeking a deeply committed relationship with a

dominant who is also my best friend. The dominance and submission should always be a part of our togetherness, although in varying degrees as best fits each individual situation. We should have great communication and rapport. We should hold each other in mutual high esteem; there should be no need to put me down for someone else to feel big. We should have great chemistry together and be open to growing what we have into love.

I want a friend I can talk to about anything and everything. We do not have to agree on things, but we should be respectful of our differences. We should be comfortable with each other even when we are silent.

Being with you should make me feel better about myself, not worse. I should be closer to self-actualizing my true self with you in my life. My well-being is important to me and it should be important to you. Your well-being is important to me, and it should be important to you. I should never be asked to do anything reckless that would endanger me. I will never be intentionally abused. That would be a red flag. It would be a reason for boundaries.

If we are really well matched with each other, we would grow well past that into a deeper level of dominance and submission. I am open to that in the right context, but not in every context; definitely not with near strangers or casual acquaintances.

My trust is earned over time. In time you prove yourself trustworthy. You do what you say when you say you will do it.

I have tried different types of relationships, but the only one that is the comfortable, good fit is the one where I am submissive to a dependable, caring dominant.

I like to cook more than I like to clean. I like to spend time out and at home. Sometimes I read a book and sometimes I watch television. Sometimes I write, take a walk, do yoga, meditate, shop or draw. I've travelled a bit and am open to a bit more. I'm always so happy to arrive back home. I've never owned a dog but I like them. I do own a lap cat. You don't have to be a parent but if you are, it's not a deal breaker for me.

I see myself as more spiritual than religious. You don't have to be either, but you could be. I do need time to devote to being close to that which I hold divine.

What kind of sub am I? I don't see myself as the type of high maintenance princess who is always putting top effort into my appearance, constantly desperate to be the center of all attention. I think I come across as a middle aged, down to earth kinkster who knows who she is, and is as comfortable in clean jeans and a t-shirt as she is in makeup and a miniskirt. I might enjoy times when I feel like your special princess, and I bask in your sincere compliments, but this is not the foundation of our relationship. I do enjoy your positive attention, and your constructively critical attention that helps me be a better me. I am educated but your level of education is not the most important thing to me. You are self-supporting, intelligent and happy with your life. I am a life-long learner and I enjoy discovering new things, people and projects.

You are comfortable in social situations. You could take the lead in a conversation (as could I) but you are also a good listener (as am I). You can communicate effectively. You are confident but not arrogant. You are kind but not weak.

So maybe you liked what you read about me. Maybe some of my key points resonated with you, but not all of them. That's okay, too.

Maybe we're the right connection. Maybe we're a possible connection.

Maybe you want to explore with me.

****

Addendum 2:
A Leading Personality Seeks His S-Partner
(This is a real person's essay. Thanks to MG.)

If I listen to my parents then the next available single person that I date is the one that I should swoop in on. That person and I should have babies and move on with life. They do know that I am not the kind to sit back and wait to be told what to do. So, nuthin' to wait for. I should give strong leadership. I should lead the next date right on into a long-term relationship. The other person, given that they are a S-type, can be expected to be pleased by my firm command. My parents will be very pleased by the number of grandchildren that our congress produces. So, it is all worked out, according to them. My personal life is set. But I am not sure that love works out that way and it is love that I want.

What isn't in my parents' expectations is love and romance. I want to be loved. I want to give my best romantic self. I want a non-egalitarian relationship model for sure but I want our non-egalitarian structure to support our great love. Can we have that? What makes me think that we can is the evidence of couples that I know firsthand. Those other couples are happy and they have been together for a long time. Can I have the right mate for me who is committed to a sustainable, long-term real thing?

I've been reading a lot about how to be a good leader and a good parent. With both I have in mind creating a kind of symbiosis. I don't want to be a dictator any more than I want to tolerate passive-aggressive behavior from my S-partner. Instead, our two personalities should fit together to take care of us. I'll do my part to watch out for where we are going long term just like what I've been reading. I'll watch out for our goals being met. I'll always be an inclusive decision maker.

You should know that anything that has to do with swimming or otherwise being in the water I'm there. I'm going to be away on trips with friends to take my boat out. I usually water ski.

I love dogs and cats but I don't usually do well with them in the house. It's best to be a sitter for friends. You know what I mean. If we lived together we could play uncle and aunt to our friend's pet so that we had a part-time dog or cat. We could talk about it. We should talk about everything.

Going out to restaurants and clubs can be fun sometimes. It's good to mix up going out and staying in. I like reading. Reading groups can be good.

You should know that I am polyamorous. It's okay if you are monogamous. All of this is worth discussing. I'm open. We would do whatever combination makes us happy. I'll do whatever we need.

I love the idea of partnering. My strongest desire is to stay clued in to my partner's desires and needs. I want my partner to be happy.

****

List of Resources

Blanchard, K. H. (2002). *Whale done!: The power of positive relationships.* New York, NY: Free Press.

De Botton, Alain. "Why You Will Marry the Wrong Person." New York

Times. http://www.nytimes.com/2016/05/29/opinion/sunday/why-you-will-marry-the-wrong-person.html?_r=0.

Hendricks, G., & Hendricks, K. (2006). *Spirit-centered relationships.* Carlsbad, CA: Hay House.

Hite, S. (1995). *The Hite report on the family: Growing up under patriarchy.* New York, NY: Grove Press.

Kaldera, R. and Joshua Tenpenny (2013). *Building the Team: Cooperative power dynamic relationships.* Hubbardston, MA: Alfred Press.

Masters, Peter (2009). *The Control Book.* Custom Books Publishing. 2nd edition.

Ed., Miller, Andrea and the editors of Shambala Sun (2011). *Right Here with You: bringing mindful awareness into our relationships.* Boston, Massachusetts: Shambala Press.

Veaux, F., & Rickert, E. (2014). *More than two: A practical guide to ethical polyamory.* Portland, OR: Thorntree Press.

****

Endnotes

[1]Masters, Peter. The Control Book. Custom Books Publishing, 2nd edition. 2009.

[2]This is just one of many articles that refers to a 2015 study out of the University of Texas at Austin and the University of California, Santa Barbara, "Men and Women Prefer Egalitarian Relationships---if Workplace Policies Support Them, http://www.huffingtonpost.com/2015/01/23/egalitarian -relationships-policies_n_6523998.html, January 23, 2015, Rebecca Adams, Huffington Post.

[3]Poster source for equality versus equity is Out Front Minnesota. Also, see a good discussion of equality versus equity in the online article, Equality is Not Enough: what the classroom has taught me about justice, Amy Sun, September 16, 2014,

http://everydayfeminism.com/2014/09/equality-is-not-enough/
and represented throughout in Kaldera's and Tenpenny's Building the Team: Cooperative Power Dynamic Relationships. Alfred Press: Hubbardston, MA. 2013.

[4]Kaldera, Raven and Joshua Tenpenny. Building the Team: Cooperative Power Dynamic Relationships. Alfred Press: Hubbardston, MA. 2013.

[5]Sparta, Kelle. See http://www.kellesparta.com/hints-for-a-happy-life/having-a-healthy-relationship/how-to-have-a-healthy-relationship-rule-1/ From one of her online healthy relationship articles her view on power dynamics leaves the partners in opposition to each other. In my opinion, this is trying to fix the Boyfriend-girlfriend scenario. I am trying to throw it out entirely. Here is a passage, which by my model is <u>not</u> an example of partnership:

First there is the issue of how we have been culturally conditioned. Every movie, book, cartoon, etc. has trained us that to be in relationship, we need to give our power over to our partner and ask for theirs in return. This is a HUGE mistake. There is rarely a reason to hand over your power to someone else. The minute you do it, you feel the loss of it. Initially the Oxytocin chemicals override your spirit's warning bells, but eventually the inevitable happens: you feel like the other person has something you need and they aren't giving it to you. This makes you clingy and needy. After all, how can you possibly be standing in your power and being solid in your being if you don't have your power? It also results in power struggles. And no one wins in a relationship power struggle because if someone wins, the relationship loses.

A Balanced Relationship Is a Healthy Relationship

Instead, you should each hold your own power. This means that you retain the responsibility to take care of your own needs, provide nurturing and care for yourself, and build your life around your own goals. If your partner does something nice for you or takes care of you in some way, this should be a bonus – not a requirement.

[6]De Botton, Alain. "Why You Will Marry the Wrong Person." New York Times article available online at http://www.nytimes.com/2016/05/29/opinion/sunday/ why-you-will-marry-the-wrong-person.html?_r=0.

[7]Hite, Shere. The Hite Report on the Family: growing up under patriarchy. New York, NY: Grove Press. 1994.

[8]McBride, Karyl. Will I Ever Be Good Enough? New York, NY: Atria Books (Simon and Schuster). 2008.

[9]You might begin with Steven Lukes, Power: a Radical View, Palgrave Macmillan, 2nd edition, 2004 and Peter Masters, The Control Book, Custom Books Publishing, 2nd edition. 2009.

[10]De Botton, Alain.

[11]This is taken from a contract that was posted and shared online for many years. I have never known the authors or succeeded in finding them but I acknowledge that I did not write this and my thanks go to those who did.

[12]See http://www.divorcestatistics.org. It reports couples with children divorce at 40% and couples without children divorce at 66% (2010). And, furthermore, 40% for first marriages, 60% for second marriages, and 74% for third marriages.

[13]BDSM Contracts. https://bdsmcontracts.org/starting-a-bdsm-relationship/

****

Unequal Partnership

www.ingramcontent.com/pod-product-compliance
Lightning Source LLC
Chambersburg PA
CBHW072134020426
42334CB00018B/1800